'*Freeing the Spirit* is ......... .......... ......... ......... ......... isdom and modern insi......... ......... ......... ......... ......... iritual journeyer.'

**Denise Linn,** author of the bestselling *Sacred Space*

'An inspiring book packed with practical exercises and spiritual insight, ideal for those trying to grow and develop to meet the challenges of the contemporary world.'

**Dr Vivianne Crowley,** Lecturer in Psychology of Religion, University of London, and author of *Wicca and Your Dark Side*

'An inspiring, caring and passionate book which brings warmth, healing and support to any spiritual traveller.'

**Leslie Kenton,** author of *Journey to Freedom*

'A rich, practical handbook for spiritual transformation and joy.'

**Robert Holden,** author of *Shift Happens!*

'A clear and engagingly written introduction to the life of the spirit, from someone who really knows the territory.'

**Starhawk,** author of *The Spiral Dance, The Twelve Wild Swans* and other books on earth-based spirituality and activism

'A really useful and practical book that applies some of the best teachings of ancient wisdom to the challenges of modern life. Full of insight and help.'

**William Bloom PhD,** author of *The Endorphin Effect*

'A joyful, brave and potent exploration into the spiritual realms – a book that is simple, but never simplistic.'

**Malcolm Stern,** psychotherapist, co-author of *The Courage to Love* and co-founder of Alternatives

'This fascinating book bridges the gap between the material and spiritual and shows in very practical ways how to invite more spirit into our everyday lives. A great book for anyone interested in transforming their life for the better.'

**Nick Williams,** author of *The Work We Were Born To Do* and founder of Heart at Work

'Steve Nobel has written a first-class explorer's guide to spirituality and personal relationships. If you've ever asked yourself "why was I born?", "what's life all about?" or "where do I go from here?", turn to Freeing the Spirit for some thoughtful and thought-provoking answers.'

**Val Sampson,** author of *Tantra: The Art of Mind-blowing Sex*

'A magical, practical and inspiring book, for all who wish to find simple ways to connect more fully with spirit in everyday life.'

**Leora Lightwoman,** founder of Diamond Light Tantra

'Steve Nobel has written a most illuminating and inspiring guide for our inner journey. His wise and compassionate teachings stir our imagination, while his useful exercises strengthen our confidence, providing inner and outer resources for the great enterprise of spiritual growth. The result is an invaluable guide for both the new and the experienced seeker, which reveals that growth can be a joyous journey with attainable goals.'

**Dr Elizabeth Puttick,** author of *Women in New Religions*

'In *Freeing the Spirit* Steve Nobel gives a most clear and concise definition of just what it means to grow as a human being. His book is a treatise on effective ways to identify our life issues and work to heal them and bring ourselves closer to wholeness (holiness). The book is full of useful practical exercises which you can undertake in your own time and which will shed light on life in all sorts of ways.'

**Leo Rutherford,** author of *Your Shamanic Path* and *Way of Shamanism*

# Freeing the Spirit

## Steve Nobel

Steve Nobel is a director of Alternatives at St James's Church in Piccadilly, London, one of the foremost venues in the UK for talks and workshops on mind, body, spirit subjects. Steve has studied many of the numerous sources of traditional wisdom that are available to people today, including martial arts, shamanism, Wicca, magic, personal development and metaphysics. He writes a regular feature for *Caduceus* magazine and runs workshops and retreats on spiritual development.

# Freeing the Spirit

Ancient & Modern Magical Techniques
to Awaken Your Inner Potential

## Steve Nobel

**RIDER**

LONDON · SYDNEY · AUCKLAND · JOHANNESBURG

1 3 5 7 9 10 8 6 4 2

First published in 2002 by Rider,
an imprint of Ebury Press, Random House
20 Vauxhall Bridge Road, London SW1V 2SA

Random House Australia (Pty) Limited
20 Alfred Street, Milsons Point, Sydney
New South Wales 2061, Australia

Random House New Zealand Limited
18 Poland Road, Glenfield
Auckland 10, New Zealand

Random House South Africa (Pty) Limited
Endulini, 5A Jubilee Road
Parktown 2193, South Africa

The Random House Group Limited Reg. No. 954009

Papers used by Rider are natural, recyclable products made from wood grown in sustainable forests.

Printed and bound by Mackays of Chatham plc, Kent.

A CIP catalogue record for this book is available from the British Library

ISBN 0-7126-1583-0

# CONTENTS

# ACKNOWLEDGEMENTS

I wish to dedicate this book to all the many guides and teachers I have met in the outer world and in the spirit worlds. I am especially grateful to Gill Edwards of Living Magically for her incredible love and wisdom over the years, to Starhawk for her courage and for her guidance into the realms of magic, to Jonathan Horowitz for his passion and compassion as a shamanic teacher and as a human being, and to Serge Kahili King for his depth of insight into the ancient wisdom of Huna.

Thank you to everyone at Alternatives, to the volunteers and people who staff the office with love. Lots of love to all the glorious and courageous Insight people (I have been so helped by your wisdom and depth of love), and may lots of blessings pour down on all the magical British Reclaiming people.

Thank you all my supportive friends: Nick, Richard, Raphaelle, Tom, British Katie now living in America and American Kate now living in Britain, and Ashley who has more talent than he currently realises. Thank you to Julia for her faith in this book and last but not least a big thank you to my greatest teachers, my children Lynda and Peter, and Ursula my Italian faerie lover and her son Ian 'the Peanut'.

# PREFACE

You may have read the book by Portia Nelson called *There's a Hole in My Sidewalk,* which has a beautifully put story that is often told and used in therapy training and personal development circles because it is a metaphor for how we can live our lives. This is my abbreviated version.

One day a person walks down a street and falls into a hole.

The next day he walks down the same street, sees the hole yet falls in again.

The next day he walks down the same street, sees the hole and walks around it.

The next day he chooses a different street.

In life there are always holes and the possibility of falling into them. There are lessons to be learnt in holes, the most important of which, often seen in hindsight, is that holes are best avoided. In life we all walk down many different streets and some of them have holes in them that we may fall into. We can fall into holes of addiction, anxiety, co-dependency, depression or madness, and such places prove generally to be very painful; however, they can also be a sort of sanctuary if the outside world appears to be very hostile and scary.

By the time I was an adolescent and adulthood was worryingly peeping over the horizon, I had fallen into a very deep hole of depression and I somehow lost my sense of purpose and direction. I dropped out of school, became quite anxious and more and more introverted and the colour seemed to be draining away from my life. Panicking, I began to seek desperately for what was wrong with me, seeking salvation first in conventional medicine, and then in more alternative approaches such as hypnosis, macrobiotics and yoga. Later I explored some forms of spirituality that I would now definitely avoid. Despite my frantic attempts to leave my hole I remained there for many years. There I blamed, suffered in silent anguish and raged about the unfairness of life. 'Why me?' I thought, 'I should have been warned.' I looked to my parents but I had little appreciation of the holes my parents had fallen into because, being British, such things were not much spoken about. In time I was to commit the same error with my own children and hide my pain and misery from them hoping that it would not hinder their chances for happiness. I was to discover that life does not work out that way.

Like some actor in a Greek tragedy I had learnt to put on many masks in order to cope. 'Well,' I thought, 'if I cannot find happiness then I will fake it.' I tried to be the perfect father, friend, husband, lover and work colleague, yet often I failed miserably. Behind my masks I seethed with anger and frustration and often this left me feeling drained of even the necessary energy to cope with life. One day I realised that I had forgotten what love felt like and felt instead only an inner icy and gaping emptiness. Although I had distant memories of the innocence of my childhood, that was long past and long lost. I felt confused about what it meant to be a man and I had a vague sense of being entangled in other people's ideas of what masculinity meant. I looked for helpful role models but found that there were few inspiring leaders or heroes around, despite the image Hollywood tried to portray.

So, confused and alone, life did not seem worth living and in my late twenties I decided to press the eject button. However, events did not go exactly to plan and instead of finding myself in the afterlife I found myself in the psychiatric unit of a London hospital. There I could at last stop pretending; my mask had slipped and for that I breathed a sigh of relief.

I remained in the psychotherapy group for several years and I met other people who also were in holes. In time I came to understand all the intricacies of my hole, how I felt being there and how I happened to fall in. But despite these insights, which did at least help me regain some compassion for myself, I remained in my hole.

In 1992, in the space of only a few months, I began to find remarkable spiritual teachers and talented healers who pointed the way to the mysterious realm of spirit. I was intrigued. I began to work with these teachers – after all, what did I have to lose? – and my worldview began to expand. I then explored working with other teachers. My life started to change, although I had to face some strong challenges first. At last I began to feel that my icy wound was beginning to heal and be filled with light. Now I am less startled by the miracles that happen in my life.

In *Freeing the Spirit* I have put together the essence of the teachings I have found most useful in the laboratory of my life. Writing the book has been not only a great joy but also a journey through all of my self-doubt and inner resistance, and as such has been one of my greatest learning experiences. The result is an attempt on my part to teach and write about that which I still most need to learn.

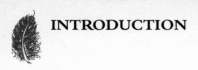# INTRODUCTION

*Freeing the Spirit* is about the art of self-transformation. It contains information and a number of techniques that can be applied to any area of life in order to bring about positive change. Areas addressed in the book include:

**Growth** – the process of stretching beyond all our limits, through our barriers of fear out into virgin territory. This process is constantly unfolding in our lives – and it is meant to be challenging.

**Spirit** – that mysterious and yet elusive force that exists within the psyche and is at the core of all life, from the smallest electron to the mightiest star. It has been sought down the ages and once felt is never forgotten; it is the great mover within all life and we would simply cease to exist if spirit stopped believing in us.

**Power** – not the kind that has long been associated with control, domination, threat and punishment, but the power that is found within. Opening to this power is like stepping into a current of energy where life becomes more juicy and vibrant.

**Magic** – the art of weaving the unseen into the seen. Every magical act can be put to creative or destructive uses, and because such acts have consequences, responsibility is needed. Magic is possible because the universe is possible.

There are many techniques and exercises in this book that seek to grant greater freedom and self-determination. Use this material responsibly and do not put aside common sense or forget to take care of yourself and your needs. Change always needs to be integrated, so do seek the counsel of friends and the help of professionals if you ever feel overwhelmed by the challenges of life.

# 1 THE MYSTERY OF GROWTH

## The Garden

*Sky-blue stillness*

*Dappled shade and sun*

*Tall trees protecting*

*Bright blooms hung*

*Amongst the abundant green.*

*Composting waste*

*Burnt ashes of pain*

*The garden becomes*

*My best teacher again*

*Cyclic shades grown green.*

Susan Hill

## What is Growth?

Down the ages many seekers have asked 'What is the purpose of life?' and the question is no less important today. The answer I have found that feels right in my heart and has proved most useful is that life is a process of growth whereby we are compelled to be and become all we can be in this lifetime. As I understand it this process of growth is all-embracing and inescapable for it encompasses every living form on the planet and includes the collective evolution of the consciousness of humanity. The wonderful thing about this process at an individual level is that as we stretch to become more than we currently experience ourselves to be, there seem to be no limits and so the process just keeps on going. Some teachers have suggested that Spirit itself is not a final product but is ever unfolding, and it unfolds through our process of growth.

It seems that everything in the universe is involved in this process, although when we look around we may be tempted to think that some people have opted out for a while, or even a lifetime. It may sometimes seem that they are moving in the opposite direction, becoming less than they can be, yet even these people cannot escape growth for long. Growth can be wonderful, joyful, scary or exciting since it involves continually extending our limits and resistances into unknown territory.

One way I understand growth is by looking at nature and at how plants and trees grow. They do not grow in a logical or linear fashion but within the context of their supportive ecosystems. In many ways we are just like seeds that wait for nature's call to send out roots and shoots. When the time is right we just have to move and leave the safety of the seed stage and begin moving through the darkness, coping with any obstacles we find on our route to the surface and the sunlight. As we grow we gain an understanding of what we are becoming – some of us may become oak trees whilst others may grow into bountiful apple trees. However, unlike trees we have choice, so if we choose to we can pull up our roots and move to a different part of the forest where the light is better and the climate and soil more to our liking. In this amazing world of action and growth we can discover all the rich potential we hold inside, and it is only when we blossom that we realise our ever unfolding potential. In my worldview this process does not start in our current lifetime but is something that has been going on over numerous lifetimes. For me birth and death are but gateways to different phases of our growth, and so both before our birth and after death we have the ability to direct our future growth. According to current metaphysical wisdom we can choose to incarnate again and choose also the circumstances of our incarnation. Choices at this level are unlike the everyday choices we make for we may choose to face very challenging circumstances in order to handle and overcome negative characteristics that have developed over many lifetimes. On the other hand we may choose positive challenges so that we can stretch into learning new skills, talents and abilities. Often we will choose to incarnate with a combination of both so that we have challenges to push against and new possibilities to pull towards. Although we have made the choices that set the stage for this lifetime, those choices may well make us feel overwhelmed and afraid. There are many strategies in life for avoiding growth and remaining safe in the seed stage. When life feels incredibly dull and predictable and we are unhappy, it is likely that we are avoiding the path of our heart and growth. Nothing is permanent in life; everything changes, and we cannot hold on to our strategies for avoiding growth for ever. Ultimately we will grow, either now or later.

## Growth and Polarity

This vast and mysterious universe contains such diversity and all of it exists within the bounds of the law of polarity. Polarity underpins how our physical universe operates since everything in existence has an opposite yet complementary state and these opposite states are in a constant dance of mutual attraction. We live in a universe of relativity where everything exists in a state that is relative to something else. Without the darkness of night we would not be able to distinguish the lights of the Milky Way; without the density of rock we would not understand the fluidity of water; without birth there could be no death; and we can experience joy only because there are states that are not joyful. There is nothing that can be conceived of that does not have an opposite and yet complementary state or quality. We so often take polarity for granted, yet if we stopped for a moment and thought about it, is it likely that this extraordinary universe arose out of a series of random molecular accidents? For me it is inconceivable that it was not designed by a higher intelligence so that all life has the opportunity to evolve and grow.

## Polarities that Exist in Life

*Birth – Death*

*Attraction – Repulsion*

*Expansion – Contraction*

*Construction – Destruction*

*Light – Darkness*

*Open – Closed*

*Inner – Outer*

*Objective – Subjective*

*Female – Male*

*Spiritual – Material*

*Conscious – Unconscious*

*Miraculous – Mundane*

*Being – Becoming*

*Love – Fear*

*Joy – Suffering*

*Compassion – Cruelty*

*Acceptance – Denial*

*Independence – Dependence*

*Expression – Suppression*

*Wholeness – Fragmentation*

It is important to note that the law of polarity has nothing to do with the judgements we make, such as what is right and wrong, since these belong purely to the human world and are not characteristics of the universe itself.

Perhaps the greatest polarity that we are here to learn to grow through is that of love and fear. Love is a part of what we are, it exists within the fabric of our soul and seeks to express itself through our bright spirit. From the quality of love all other soul qualities arise. A soul quality could be described as something that makes our body smile when it is felt and expressed, such as freedom, joy, enthusiasm, compassion and wisdom. These qualities are developed through an experiential awareness and understanding of their opposite pole, so in order to understand and know compassion the lessons of cruelty must be understood and assimilated. Similarly, for wisdom there is ignorance, for clarity there is confusion, for connection there is alienation, and for joy there is suffering. These restrictive tendencies are the challenges of the physical universe that serve to awaken the full expression of the soul qualities that lie dormant within us. Fear exists in the physical universe only so that we may know love. Fear is the challenge we will inevitably face when on a path of growth, for fear is a part of the great illusion of this world and its main purpose is to help us remember love.

## Growth is Always Challenging

*Then the time came*
*when the risk it took*
*to remain tight in a bud*
*was more painful than*
*the risk it took to blossom.*

Anaïs Nin

Life is meant to be challenging. This is not to say that life has to be hard or difficult or a struggle or painful, simply that it is meant to be challenging so that we are motivated to stretch beyond the familiar into virgin territory and thus awaken and discover more of who we truly are. Challenge means many things to many people and it is important to know how you define challenge since this will fundamentally affect your experience of it. Since challenge exists within polarity it will be experienced either as a push out of a familiar situation or a pull towards something new. The former would involve some kind of loss or ending, such as the death of someone close, divorce or redundancy, and the latter would involve some kind of gain or new beginning, such as a birth in the family, a new relationship or the beginning of a new business or project. Whichever form it takes, challenge is there to help us awaken dormant abilities, talents and soul qualities that may be slumbering within us and, like Sleeping Beauty, await the magical kiss from some passing challenge to wake them up. Yet at some level we all have an inbuilt resistance to growth, with the nature of this resistance depending on our level of awareness of it. Unconscious resistance to change tends to manifest as physical symptoms (tiredness or aches and pains), emotional turbulence (sudden bouts of fear), or mental anxiety (doubt and confusion).

Growth always involves some sort of change, yet there is a danger that we may become a growth addict, so goal orientated that we forget it is the journey rather than the destination that is important and never stop to smell the roses along the way.

Malcolm Stern came through public school not really knowing what he wanted to do. After a stint in accountancy he became an estate agent, which he thought was a 'radical move' at the time. During this time Malcolm went through a number of challenging life events, including being stalked by a woman for four years. The stress and anxiety of this period caused his physical health to deteriorate and he began to realise that his lifestyle had to change. His journey took him into counselling and group therapy. He went to work for Greenpeace for two years and spent some time on the ship *Rainbow Warrior*. In 1979 he attended the World Symposium on Humanity and discovered there that his life was about service. Malcolm went on to train as a psychotherapist and to write a book on relationships. He helped to co-found Alternatives, a London-based non-profit organisation promoting mind/body/spirit events, and now says that he is 'happy to be used by life'.

Challenge can involve doing something that is just a small step beyond our comfort zone, or it can be a great leap of faith that really tests us. It is challenging to be a parent, to have parents, to move to a new area, to change career, to begin meditating or to follow a vision. Challenge may come as a consequence of actions we have taken in the past or it can come in the form of a crisis, which can be a time of both threat and great possibility. Challenges can, of course, be fun, joyful and freeing – and ways to expand our self-confidence and self-esteem. It can be challenging and thrilling to speak our truth, 'walk our talk' and step upon the path of our heart and follow our dreams. It can be challenging to step away from the crowd and find our own truth and path rather than simply following others. It can be challenging to break out of limiting cultural values or a rigid sense of personal identity and step into the unknown. Facing challenge and handling it will inevitably lead to a greater sense of inner power. However, growth is a powerful process because it is also a risky one. There are no guarantees along the way; we may plot a course to a particular destination yet life will always throw up the unexpected. The element of uncertainty allows challenge to be very real and unpredictable.

A fellow director at Alternatives, Tom Cook, spent 28 years as a television director, producer and executive in New York, Sydney, Auckland and London. After experiencing a rare type of hepatitis he realised, at the age of 49, that what he really wanted to do was devote the rest of his life to becoming an artist, something he had no training for. Although a part of him considered this to be a mad idea, he followed his creative dream. The transition was not an easy one, but Tom was soon painting and selling pictures as well as holding art workshops in order to help others get in touch with their creativity.

Make the decision to chart a course and steer your life out into the unexplored territories of your psyche to discover more about who you are and could be. This is a journey that we must all take, and we can go either kicking and screaming or singing and dancing along the way.

## Growth Through Joy or Suffering

*The gentle spring rain permeates the soil of my soul.*
*A seed that has lain deeply in the earth for many years just smiles.*
Thich Nhat Hanh

Sometimes it can seem as if life must be difficult and include large doses of pain and suffering. We are all used to hearing 'no pain no gain' and 'suffering is good for the soul', and many of us have had harsh experiences that have been full of pain and suffering. Pain can be a powerful motivator, and for some people it is the only one. Modern-day living so easily generates considerable stress and pain that we can be fooled into believing that this is the only way life can be. Pain may seem a better option than feeling nothing at all, and a life full of drama may seem more attractive than a life filled with boredom. Qualities such as courage and success have long been tested and developed through arenas of conflict and pain and we can forget that they can be developed in other ways also. The Buddha taught about the nature and cessation of suffering, but I was never able to absorb fully the first noble truth of Buddhism that 'All life is suffering'. Then a few years ago, whilst participating in a workshop not related to Buddhism, an inner voice said 'the first noble truth is that suffering exists'. After the workshop I did some research and found a Buddhist teacher who taught this message. Thich Nhat Hanh, a Vietnamese Zen teacher living in exile in France, dismisses the idea that the Buddha taught that everything is suffering. Instead, he interprets the first noble truth as saying that suffering simply exists. He points out that because the Buddha spoke an ancient dialect of the Indian language and his words have never been recorded in his own mother tongue, his teachings have been exposed to the dangers of mistranslation and misinterpretation.

There are many things that generate suffering – an inability to let go of the past, a refusal to forgive, being caught in delusion and fantasising about the future as a way of escaping the present, being locked in a feeling of being needy or valueless, being stuck in judgement, being highly self-critical and feeling that life has no meaning. By believing in the necessity of suffering we lock ourselves into a mindset where life and growth must be bound with suffering. Naturally a refusal to confront difficult or painful feelings is also likely to lead to suffering. Only pain embraced and accepted has the potential to be transformed.

On the other hand joy needs to be cultivated, for it grows in the fertile soil of trust, self-love and a sense of freedom. Joy comes from choices that support such a state no matter what choices other people are making in their lives. Growing with joy does not mean always appearing to be happy or seeking to hide any difficult feelings; rather, it is being authentic, being in the present moment and honestly expressing whatever is in our hearts. Opening to and expressing inner potential leads to joy. The joyous state is an inner state, not dependent on any of the 'false idols' in the world. Joy is a gateway to inspiration; it looks at how life could be. Feeling and expressing joy can break the habitual thought patterns that produce feelings of being stuck and unhappy in a world where pain and suffering seem so prevalent. Growing with joy means that life can become an exciting adventure rather than a daily slog. Doesn't that sound more appealing?

Joy can be blocked by a number of things, such as guilt. Can we really allow ourselves to feel joyful knowing that there is so much suffering in the world? Although being joyful in such a world can feel like a betrayal, joy is the greatest gift we can give for it shows another way to be and experience the world. Joy can be expressed through just a gentle smile or a kind touch or through a wild dance or passionate song. Joy is the natural state of our soul; it is our inheritance and as such is meant to be expressed in the world.

## Choose Joy

- Each morning when you wake up, consciously choose joy – and no matter what happens throughout the day, continue to choose it.

- Place your attention on noticing the joy in the world and actively seek it out in every moment.

- Have you noticed that joyful people are naturally more attractive? Make a point of finding out what makes other people joyful.

- If being in nature brings you joy then spend time each day in nature.

- If being creative, such as painting or singing, brings you joy then give yourself some time each day to explore this.

- Keep a journal where you can note down your daily encounters with joy.

# Meditations

*Freeing the Spirit* includes a number of meditations. There are a few general points to note here so that you can be well prepared before any are attempted.

1  You will need to find a space where you will not be disturbed for a set period of time. This space will need to have a feeling of serenity and stillness. You can if you like light a candle each time you meditate. These meditations can be done either in silence or with ambient music, as you prefer.

2  Intention is everything so it is important to be clear on the purpose of the meditation. Read it through a number of times to get clear on its vital points. You can have a friend guide you through the meditation or you can record it on tape and play it back as you are meditating. Alternatively there are CDs available on some of the meditations found here (see page 204 for further information). These meditations involve closing the eyes and opening the inner eye of the imagination and using a variety of visualisation techniques.

3  In regard to posture these meditations can be done either sitting or lying down. It is important that the chest is open so that breathing is unrestricted and also that the spine is relatively straight.

4  The meditations begin and end with awareness of the ongoing cycle of breath. Yogis say that the in-breath and the out-breath are the two guards of the city of life. Breath is a reflection of our state of being, and so when we are tense or frightened our breathing is very different from our breathing when we are joyful or serene. Awareness of the breath is a very ancient technique and can be used for becoming more present, for increasing life-force energy or simply for signalling to the body consciousness that meditation practice is about to begin.

5  With awareness of the breath you may find that you enter a place of stillness and peace, or you may find that you are more aware of the

restlessness of the mind. In the latter case this may occur because your mind is over-stimulated and not used to this kind of practice. However, with practice and perseverance, and without fighting, the mind can be harnessed and its energy directed towards the focus of the meditation.

## A Meditation on Joy and Suffering

*Find a posture where your spine is straight and close your eyes and become aware of the cycle of your breath. Without changing how you breathe notice your natural rhythm and watch your in-breath – the pause – the out-breath – the pause. Do not interfere with or attempt to control your breathing, simply notice it, placing your full attention on this cycle. Although thoughts and feelings may arise in you, simply notice them and bring your attention back to the breath. Accept where you are with this process and continue to place your full awareness on the breath.*

*Now spend some time dwelling on suffering. Fix your attention on the feeling of suffering and what it means to you. Allow any images, thoughts, memories or feelings of suffering to arise. Stay centred and focused and do not allow yourself to become lost in your stream of consciousness; stay present and still, mindful of your breath. This simple awareness of your suffering is a step towards healing. Then when you are ready, give permission for all the suffering within you to diminish. See it shrinking so that you can hold it as a ball of pulsing energy in your hand. See it shrink to the size of a marble, and then of a pea, and then of a grain of sand – and then it is gone.*

*Then spend some time dwelling on joy. Fix your attention on the thought of joy and what it means to you. Allow any images, memories or feelings of joy to arise. Do not get lost in this stream of consciousness; stay conscious of your breath and the joy that is within you.*

*When you are ready, give this joy permission to increase and allow it to expand and fill your body, mind and emotions. Become filled with the feeling of joy until you are a radiant star sending out joy to everything and everyone around you.*

*With your awareness of your cycle of breath, slowly come back to full waking consciousness.*

## Growth Through Inner and Outer Power

Power is an essential quality for growth and it can act both as a propelling force and a limiting one. Power either threatens to ensnare us from the outside or it radiates out through us from our spiritual core.

The Threatening Face of Power is rooted in a deep sense of feeling powerless in life and in the conviction that all power exists outside of the self. We are often conditioned to believe that power primarily exists within such things as multinational corporations, organised religion, governments, the scientific establishment, the military, and so on. Such bodies appear so powerful and we seem so small in comparison. We can also get caught up in thinking that if only we could know enough, look good enough, be strong enough, be connected enough, be critical enough, be aggressive enough or manipulative enough then somehow we could get to be powerful too. Such modes of power are based in fear and have little belief in inner power, or if they do they see it as an aggressive force to be used to dominate others. Such a worldview sees power as a scarce commodity where only a select few can wield the baton of authority, and so often power must be taken by stealth, force or deceit. Naturally, all of this is a recipe for conflict, which in turn will generate victims and persecutors and, inevitably, pain and suffering. Life then becomes a battlefield of winners or losers; some even see this conflict continuing into the afterlife, with the winners going to somewhere nice and the losers ending up somewhere horrible for eternity. Such ideas have tended to be responsible for the violence, warfare and mayhem on our planet.

The Radiant Face of Power is rooted in a state of internal connectedness and an appreciation of the spirit that dwells within. This power flows from our core out into the world and allows for an aligning and harnessing of all our physical, emotional, mental and spiritual resources towards upliftment and growth. This inner power is friendly yet it is also unpredictable, for it seeks to sweep us beyond the safety of the known and out into the great mystery of our unknown potential. This inner power seeks to make us a vehicle for change in the world and to engage us in issues where transformation is needed. This power sees no enemies, only a flow of inter-connectedness – since we are all connected through spirit – and visions to be supported. This power flows through the gap between our thoughts and manifests in our words and actions on our life's path. Without this power we would cease to exist, for it ever sustains us and creates us anew. Paradoxically this power is also to be found within our vulnerability, for it is here that are found the gems of gentleness, playfulness and innocence. It is also, strangely enough, to be found within the things we fear the most. There is a saying in witchcraft that goes 'where there is fear there is power', and this is because fear is an energy that has the potential to be useful. Fear is where our energy is at its most contracted, and liberating any internal patterns of fear creates a greater amount of mental, emotional and physical energy for more positive uses.

Our power resides in the core of our spirit, which could be defined, if such a thing were possible, as the divine indwelling soul and the intelligence that creates and sustains the universe anew in each and every moment.

## A Meditation on Inner Power

*Begin to relax and be aware of your breath.*

*Relax physically by being aware of any tension in your body and, with awareness, ask your body to relax. You can tense parts of your body and then relax them to notice the difference if this helps.*

*Notice your breath and use the polarity of the inward and outward breath to take you deeper in relaxation. Do not interfere with the breath, simply be aware of it. In this state notice all your thoughts and feelings and allow them to be whatever they are.*

*Within your body is a point where you feel the most centred and tranquil. This may be in the heart or belly regions. Explore where you feel most centred. You will know this place when you find it by the sense of peace and tranquillity that is there.*

*This is also your place of power and you can open to this inner power and allow it to flow through you as if there is a fountain of energy that is beginning to pour forth from you. Being mindful of your breath, allow this power to radiate throughout your physical body; allow it to be absorbed into your bones, your blood, your organs, your muscles, tissue and skin. Feel the whole physical body absorbing this pure energy and then allow this power to flow into your emotions. Feel this pure sparkling energy stream through your emotions. As you feel this energy allow it to flow into those places that hold your anger, envy, hostility, grief and pain. Allow this inner power to liberate the power locked in your emotions and let this energy flow.*

*Then allow this power (it can be either a calming or an invigorating force) to flow into your mind. Allow it to stream into all the places in your mind where your energy is locked into limiting your thinking patterns. Allow this energy to begin to disentangle itself and add to the flow of power passing through your mind. Stay in this flow as long as you wish, then come back to your centre of power and begin to be aware of your breath. When you are ready, return to full waking consciousness refreshed and alive and ready to meet the day.*

## Making and Breaking Masks of Power

For this exercise you will need a piece of card or paper big enough to cover your face. A paper plate will do if there is nothing else to hand. With this you can make a mask that represents all the threatening aspects of power you have experienced in your life. Into this mask you can pour all the abuse and hurt and situations where you have felt people have had power over you. Gather some art materials – crayons, paint, feathers, beads, coloured wool, glue, glitter, and whatever else you wish. Before you begin to make this mask, spend some time in meditation recalling all the times you have felt threatened and bullied and controlled. What feelings do you have about the abuse of power? When you are ready, allow the emotions that are bottled up inside you to pour out into the mask as you make it. If any words come to mind then simply speak these into the mask. Take your time and when you are finished sit with your mask and feel the power of it. You can either keep this mask as a reminder of the work you still want to do around this issue or, if you are ready, you can choose to burn it in a sacred ceremony to celebrate being free of what it represents. This exercise can be done alone or as a group activity.

On a different occasion repeat this exercise but this time make a mask that represents the positive and radiant aspects of power that you wish to invite into your life. This mask can be placed somewhere in your home or garden to remind you of your radiant inner power.

## Expressing Power Safely

For thousands of years across the planet it has not been safe to express inner power, and countless people have been hurt, rejected or killed for speaking their truth or acting with integrity. Just as a child will learn to feel afraid of fire after being burnt, so too on a larger scale we have learnt to play small in life. It is generally safe now, at least in the Western world, to allow this inner power to radiate out and touch others. Opening to inner power will inevitably lead to a more empowering way of living, and the world now needs people to help anchor this new vibration of inner power. As more of us embrace our inner power with gentleness and wisdom, old limiting power structures cannot help but collapse, making way for more enlightened channels for this radiant power.

# 2 THE POWER OF THE CONSCIOUS MIND

*Energy is eternal delight.*

William Blake

Modern-day living can so easily condition us to be 'heady', with the intellect always on the go. Like a machine that cannot be turned off, the mind rarely seems to rest. Even as we wake up the intellect is already in gear, scanning the papers over breakfast for information, planning the day ahead, making mental adjustments to the day's demanding schedule, remembering appointments to keep and other important matters that require consideration. As we shall see, this tendency to live through an overactive intellect represents an unbalanced approach to life. This is likely to lead to a constant internal mental chattering that can in turn lead to unhappiness, stress and, if taken too far, eventual breakdown. Although the abilities of the mind are great they were not designed to cope with such a lopsided and punishing workload. There is a Zen story about a man on a galloping horse. It appears that he is going somewhere important. A man standing by the road shouts, 'Where are you going?' and the rider replies, 'I don't know! Ask the horse!'

## The Polarities Within the Conscious Mind

Research has shown that there are two hemispheres of the brain that house very different functions of the mind. The left hemisphere seems to control the right side of the body and the functions of logic, language and the separating function of the intellect. The more mysterious right hemisphere seems to control the left side of the body and relates to feelings, intuition, spatial perception, receptivity and a more holistic way of perceiving life. In Western culture the 'left-brain' way of being is usually favoured and is thus more dominant in people's lives. Western society tends to value and financially reward those individuals who are able to analyse, calculate, think logically, be dynamic, problem solve and generally handle the objective world successfully. Right-brain people on the other hand – the artists, dreamers, mystics, storytellers and poets – are often looked down on and sometimes even shunned by society.

It is my understanding that these two polarities arise from much deeper archetypal masculine and feminine energies that are held within the blueprint of the psyche. Carl Jung, one of the great pioneers of psychology who sailed into the realms of consciousness, called these archetypal energies the Anima and Animus, and he felt that every human being, regardless of gender, had access to them both. In order to understand the different functions of the conscious mind I have personified the two sides of my conscious mind, calling my 'left-brain' self the Inner Warrior and my 'right-brain' self the Inner Priestess. This has helped me to make these two aspects more accessible and open up new ways of connecting with them. The Warrior can also be seen as female and the Priestess as male. Thus the former could be a figure like Queen Boudicea of ancient Britain or a goddess figure like Artemis the Huntress of ancient Greece, and the latter could be a figure such as Merlin the Wise of Arthurian Britain, or Orpheus who journeyed to the underworld to rescue his beloved Eurydice.

## The Interference of Stereotypes

Beliefs about gender can often get in the way of how we relate to these two modes of consciousness. Modern societies are largely built upon older patriarchal structures that defined masculine energy as being superior to feminine energy. For too long men have been conditioned to be strong and to avoid displaying any kind of vulnerability; similarly, women have been conditioned to see themselves as fit only for mothering or domestic duties. Such ideas have created great internal distortions in our collective psyche and affect the ways in which we feel, see and express our Priestess and Warrior energies.

I once attended a personal development course which encouraged participants to explore the stereotypical ideas they held about the opposite gender. When lunchtime came we were divided into groups of four – two men and two women – and instructed to speak and act as if we were of the opposite sex. This was a particularly challenging exercise for me because the other male in my group was a well-known TV comedian who specialised in impersonating women. Over lunch the men acting as women discussed shopping and fashion and cooed over all the babies and children in the restaurant. The women acting as men discussed football, ferrets and sex and lusted after anyone who was female. It was a hilarious yet challenging exercise, especially when we had to go out onto the streets of Leeds and walk as we imagined the opposite gender did. After doing this exercise most people became aware that the character they had portrayed was a stereotype, because they lacked a real understanding of how the opposite gender saw and experienced life.

When masculine and feminine energies are overlaid with culturally accepted ideas that seek to restrict their full range of expression within the psyche, some aspects can get exaggerated and others damped down. In some cases restrictive ideas about gender can serve to suppress one side, leaving it almost unavailable in daily life and causing the remaining side to carry the full workload.

## *Ask Yourself*

*Take a look at your family's influence upon your ideas of masculine and* feminine energies. How limiting or expansive were the views expressed there?

What influence did your religious or cultural background have in shaping your ideas?

What experiences helped you shape your ideas about what it means to be a man or a woman?

What do you see as the main differences between the masculine and the feminine?

What do you find challenging about either?

## The Priestess

> *You are the happy mother of the stars.*
>
> *You sink down in the perilous ocean*
>
> *Without harm and without hurt*
>
> *You rise up on the quiet wave*
>
> *Like a young queen in flower.*
>
> Traditional Irish Gaelic prayer

The Priestess is the Yin or the receptive and soft side of our mind that is seated in the right hemisphere of the brain. She is poised to receive a stream of information from the unconscious mind and she is connected with the heart. She is the feeling self that can peer beneath surface reality to the realms of the unseen, who hears the soft language of the soul that whispers to her through the inner realms. She is the part of us which knows the qualities that lie dormant within – and she can call to them to awaken in life. She is the still and reflective side of the conscious mind and in her we can find much needed rest from the frantic activity of our lives. Like the Sumerian goddess Innana, the Priestess knows the way through the underworld of the psyche and is able to pass through the gates that bar the way. She hears the parts of us that call for integration and she can feel the wounds of the soul. She carries no weapons and so is defenceless and open. Her main powers are imagination and vision, which she uses to operate in the inner realms of subjective reality. She can be called on in life and is most active in the dream state.

## Resistance to the Priestess

The Priestess has been greatly maligned, distrusted and misunderstood in our world for she operates at levels of consciousness that are beyond the narrow range of the logical mind. Her powers have largely been discarded and declared useless by society, which now prizes the intellect and objective reality above all else. When her resources retreat and become unavailable, a feeling of internal disconnection arises and we cut off from our body, our emotions and the light of our soul and spirit. In life this is like sailing across an ocean with no radar or sonar systems for guidance.

Resistance to the Priestess stems from a basic fear of feminine energy or from the absence of a 'good enough' mothering figure early on in life.

Lucy lost her mother when she was 14, 'exactly at the moment I was about to start the transition into womanhood, so my entry was unguided, lonely, guesswork, uncertain, almost unwanted and certainly scarier than it would have been had my mother been alive'. Lucy was brought up by her father and later went to boarding school. She grew up with a very strong Warrior, which manifested itself as a strong sense of independence. She could very easily produce long lists of goals to achieve and was constantly driving herself on to the next challenge. She had an impressive academic CV yet complained that she never felt good enough or never knew what she really wanted to do in life. In an inner journey to go and meet the Priestess, Lucy connected to the grief she felt when her mother left her at such an early age. When she discovered that the Priestess just was not there, she determined that a part of her work in this lifetime would be to call the Priestess back.

There is evidence to suggest that our long distant ancestors saw the Spirit of All Things as female, possibly because it made more sense to see a goddess figure giving birth and sustaining a universe than a male one. Gradually this view changed to the opposite extreme and the feminine face of the Divine was banished. We now live under the shadow of an all-powerful father-like figure that rules the cosmos with an unforgiving hand. Increasingly the earth is seen less as a sacred and nurturing place and more as a testing ground of good and evil. The cosmos somehow became split into heaven and hell, spirit and matter, saints and sinners. The feminine also split, into the pure virginal or nurturing side and the dark, lustful and even evil side. This split needs to be healed so that we can regain the amazing abilities of the Priestess.

## A Meditation for Invoking the Priestess

*Find some time to be alone and sit in silence, perhaps lighting a candle and dedicating it to awakening your Inner Priestess. It may be useful to have an image that represents the Priestess, such as a tarot card of the High Priestess/Empress or an image of a goddess, or perhaps something like a seashell, a small crystal or a flower.*

*Decide that you would like to meet and experience the Priestess within. Notice any apprehension you may have, and if there is any just imagine that you can put it aside for the time being and address it later.*

*Close your eyes and begin to be aware of your breath. Allow any tension to flow out of you on the out-breath, and on the in-breath imagine you are breathing a white light into your lungs. Again on the out-breath visualise yourself letting go of any tension. Continue breathing in light and releasing any tension until you are totally relaxed and feel your whole body filled with white light. Open yourself to feeling the innocence of your being in this light.*

*Imagine that you can turn away from the outside world and begin to open to your inner world. Open all your inner senses and gradually allow yourself to be in a scene in nature. Allow this scene to be however it presents itself – a lush green place; a warm, watery, exotic setting or perhaps a rocky landscape – trust your first impressions. Do not worry if your vision of this place is vague and misty at first; you may be feeling it through one of your other senses such as touch or smell, or you may just feel it in your heart. With practice scenes in the inner world will become sharper and can feel every bit as real as the outer world.*

*Enjoy being in your inner world and notice how you feel; begin to explore this landscape and go in search of a place where you can meet your Inner Priestess. In this place mentally call to her and wait until she is ready to come to you. See her in the distance walking towards you and as she draws nearer notice everything you can about her – her general appearance, the colour of her hair, and her clothes and jewellery. As she draws near notice how you feel in her presence. Allow yourself to be surprised by how she looks. For now simply greet her and sit with her, feel her presence radiating out to you. Trust your initial impressions and accept her however she appears. If she seems a powerful figure then allow her to send out energy to you and be open to receive it, for this energy is a gift that can be useful in the outer world. If you wish, explain to her that you are ready to express her energy more fully in your life, then listen to anything she wants to say to you. She may present you with a symbolic gift that represents a quality she is ready to bring to you. If you wish, accept this gift and absorb its energy into your body.*

*If your Priestess appears wounded then just sit with her.*

*Stay with her for as long as you want and when you are ready to return, thank your Inner Priestess and go back through the landscape the way you came. When you are ready to become aware once more of your breath, the landscape will simply dissolve into a fine mist. You then come back to full waking consciousness.*

## The Warrior

*You are what your deep driving desire is,*

*As your desire, so is your will.*

*As your will, so is your deed.*

*As is your deed, so is your destiny.*

Baghavad Gita

The Warrior is the Yang or dynamic and assertive side of our mind that is seated in the left hemisphere of the brain. He stands ready to build, commit, act, plan, structure, assess, choose, converse, engage, design, think, set boundaries, speak and generally do anything you want. The Warrior comes fully armed with a probing intellect, which is used to separate reality out into understandable chunks. He also has a shield that is used to defend all vulnerability within the psyche. The Warrior is our personal will which naturally seeks to be on the move, striving for greater levels of achievement and new challenges. This is our bold and courageous side, essential for turning our visions into reality. The Warrior has the power of commitment, focus and determination, and he is capable of incisive thought and independent action. This is where our courage, individuality and nobility lie, and where he is absent we find it difficult to set goals or take any meaningful or powerful action to manifest our reality. This is like having a ship with no means of propulsion. The Warrior generally feels more comfortable operating in the outer world of objective reality, although he is able to journey in shamanic fashion into the inner worlds.

## Resistance to the Warrior

Throughout the last several thousand years there has been an excess of masculine energy on the planet, because patriarchal cultures have tended to elevate qualities classified as masculine (such as the separating intellect) over those qualities classified as feminine (such as the connecting power of intuition). This has tended to lead to the development of systems of control and domination on the planet, with war as the main consequence. This has caused the Warrior to be used in ways that are cold, brutal and violent – a distortion of the Warrior's true nature. The Warrior cannot handle tasks that are the natural domain of the Priestess, and he needs her guidance. In our present world many either use the Warrior energy in inappropriate ways or they seek to disown it because they blame it for all the bloodshed and 'evil' on the planet. When the Warrior is disowned, issues of boundaries and effectiveness in life always arise. Without the inner masculine to set boundaries, focus, plan and take action on the guidance of the Priestess, nothing very juicy is going to happen.

Resistance to the Warrior can stem from a basic fear and distrust of masculine energy and can be rooted in either the absence of a 'good enough' fathering figure or the presence of a strongly dysfunctional father figure during the formative years.

Elisabeth grew up in a household where her father left when she was six. She remembered her father as prone to uncontrollable angry outbursts, and although she stayed in touch with him she knew him only as a distant, bullying figure. She now lives with her mother and although they love each other very much Elisabeth often feels overwhelmed by her mother's demands. Recently Elisabeth became allergic to many different foods and her immune system was having difficulty in coping with life. In an inner journey we went to meet the Warrior and found him to be a pale and ghostly figure. Her work now is to call back the Warrior.

## A Meditation for Invoking the Warrior

*Find some time for this meditation in the morning and sit in silence. It may be useful to have an image before you that represents the Inner Warrior, such as a tarot card of the Charioteer or Emperor or an image of masculine energy such as a warrior figurine or an image of the sun or a stag.*

*Become aware of the growing light and power of the rising sun.*

*Choose to meet and experience the Warrior within and notice any apprehension you may feel. Now simply let it go and close your eyes and begin to be aware of your breath. Allow any tension to flow out of you on the out-breath, and on the in-breath imagine you are breathing a golden light into your lungs. Allow your whole body to be filled and bathed with this golden light, and feel the power and strength of this light increasing. Begin to open to your inner world and allow a scene of nature to rise up gently around you. See, smell, feel, hear and touch this place, trusting your first impressions. Notice how you feel in this landscape. When you are ready, begin to explore it and find a place where you can meet your Inner Warrior. Mentally call to the Warrior to come and join you and watch him gradually make his way towards you. As he draws nearer notice everything you can about him. Finally, as he stands before you, notice how you feel in his presence. If you feel he is a powerful figure, allow him to send out his power towards you. Accept this energy, if you wish; it is a gift that can be taken and used in the outer world. If you wish, explain to him that you are ready to express his energy more fully in your life, then listen to anything he wants to say to you. He may present you with a symbolic gift representing a quality he is ready to bring to you. If you wish, accept this gift and absorb its energy into your body.*

*If the Warrior feels wounded in some way then just stay with him. Stay as long as you want and when you are ready to return, thank your Inner Warrior and go back through the landscape until you become aware once more of your breath. The inner landscape will dissolve into a fine mist as you step back towards full waking consciousness.*

## Going Deeper

### The Priestess

The Priestess is the part of us that is connected to our soul and spirit. Through her we receive inspiration, purpose and insight, and these qualities are then used to direct the energy of the Warrior. The Priestess receives guidance and the Warrior acts upon that guidance. This only works when we have faith in our Priestess mind. Now it is time to open up to the possibilities that the Priestess brings.

### Engaging the Priestess

To engage the Priestess:

+ Spend time in nature – try out different places such as forests or the seashore, or perhaps visit a sacred site such as Avebury in

Wiltshire and connect with the stones there. Try gazing at the moon or the stars and breathe in their light.

◆ Stare into a dancing candle flame or a crystal sphere with a gentle, soft gaze and allow images to arise from your unconscious. Try this also with a painting, a flower or a tarot card.

◆ Find solitude and stillness and get to know yourself.

◆ Begin to notice and record your dreams, read fairy stories, poetry and magical books, or try some ecstatic dancing.

◆ Open to your creativity and find ways to access the voice of your imagination. Allow images to float into your consciousness; play with them and find the power they contain.

◆ Tune into your innermost feelings and try writing them out using your non-dominant hand.

If you have any difficulty in meditating on the Priestess it may be that your body is too tense or your mind is holding too much turbulent energy. Find ways to relax and release any tension. Try taking a long bath or go for a massage or a counselling session. Take some time away from being busy for a while.

## Intuition

*Intuition is the Priestess's ability to access and know information that is not readily available to the intellect. Intuition could also be called instinct, a gut feeling, or a sudden flash of insight. Intuition is a useful skill that occurs on many levels, and it can be developed. Simply bring yourself to a still place and hold your attention on a difficult decision, situation or person. Notice how you feel at each level of your being. Give yourself some space and sufficient time to allow the whole range of your intuition to speak. Intuition operates on four levels:*

◆ *The physical – at this level intuition is felt within the body itself, where feelings of tightness and tension or of lightness and expansion are messages. Does your body smile or cringe in response?*

◆ *The emotional – because intuition also acts at an emotional level, always take into account your feelings about a certain topic. Are they light and pleasant or heavy and unpleasant in response?*

◆ *The mental – intuition can also happen through imagery. What images arise in your mind's eye? Are they bright or fearful in response?*

◆ *The Spiritual – open to the light of spirit and feel its guidance through your heart. What does your heart say?*

## A Meditation to Awaken the Radiant Heart of the Priestess

Sit quietly in a space where you will not be disturbed and simply experience being still.

Allow your mind to become as calm as a mountain lake under an evening sky.

Place your attention on the cycle of your breath and use it to become more relaxed. Allow any stress or tension simply to dissolve like mist. Imagine with each out-breath you are releasing any tension. If your attention wanders off, simply acknowledge this and return to the breath.

Place your awareness in your heart and imagine you can breathe in and out of your heart. Breathe the light of love into your heart on the in-breath and feel your heart opening to this love as if it were a flower. Breathe in the light of love from the universe and fill your heart with a golden pink light. At a certain point the amount of light in your heart is so great it begins to spill out and flow into your body. Allow your body to drink in the light of this love and then allow it to spill into your emotions where it is absorbed, calming any turbulence there. Then the light begins to *flow into your mind and is absorbed into its very fabric.*

*When you are filled with this light, imagine sending it to people and situations in the world that are in need of this love.*

*When you are ready, come back to your heart and from there return to everyday consciousness through your awareness of the breath. Keep this feeling of love in your heart and enjoy it consciously throughout the day or in the dream state.*

## The Warrior

The Warrior is polished and developed in the fire of life's challenges and experiences. As long as he is connected to the guiding light of the Priestess all will be well. For too long Warrior energy has been used to suppress and limit the power of the Priestess. He is always most effective when he follows her guidance, otherwise he tends to be directed by the most negative parts of our nature. Invite the Warrior into your life and engage his abilities well.

## The Power of Commitment

+ Choose an area of your life where you wish to make some changes.

+ Decide whether you are willing to commit to making changes in this area.

+ Become clear on how you would like this area of your life to be.

+ See where you have given away your inner authority and power to others in this area.

+ Commitment is a place of power where tangible and achievable steps can be made to change a situation. Place this commitment in a timeframe such as, 'Within one week I will donate $x$ amount of money to a charity to help the environment', or 'Today I will call my friend whom I haven't called for ages'. Only make a commitment where you feel willing and able to carry it through. Check your level of enthusiasm for taking some positive steps in the world. If any fear comes up around fulfilling your commitment, simply breathe through it and allow the energy that the fear contains to be redirected into helping you fulfil your intentions.

◆ Keeping a commitment journal may be helpful. Avoid committing to something out of a sense of obligation, for if you do not feel passionate about completing the commitment then not doing so will only reinforce any feelings of failure or lack of self-worth.

## A Meditation on the Power of Focus

*Choose something that you would like to allow more of into your life, such as freedom, love, joy, passion or clarity. Choose an image that represents this quality for you – perhaps a soaring eagle for freedom or a rose quartz heart for love. Once you have chosen an image and feel comfortable with it, begin to visualise it intensely. Notice the power of the symbol and play with it. Place it within an appropriate setting: for example, see your eagle soaring through a vibrant blue sky over a great pine forest.*

*After you have set the image in motion allow the symbol to do whatever it wants, so let your eagle sweep across this sky to head towards distant mountains if it so wishes. Just follow the symbol and see what happens. Play with your symbol and allow it to do the unexpected, even changing form if it wishes. If any fear creeps into your visualisation simply be aware of it and use it to enhance your journey with your symbol. So, for example, if an archer is shooting at the eagle from below, have your eagle swoop down and see him off. Keep your focus on this symbol; if you find yourself distracted simply bring your attention back to this exercise.*

*Allow the symbol to evoke the feeling you desire within yourself. When you are ready, bring your symbol into your heart and simply imagine its energy merging into you.*

*Try this visualisation on one symbol for at least ten minutes each day for one week before changing to another.*

## Engaging the Warrior

To become more open to the Warrior:

◆ Take up cooking, gardening, martial arts, painting, swimming, walking or, perhaps, passionate dancing such as Salsa.

◆ Do something that engages the mind such as planning your day, checking your accounts, thinking about a decision you need to make or reading a book.

◆ Try making a commitment to do something that you have been putting off doing, and then simply keep it.

◆ Enjoy the art of thinking and communicating and practise the art of relating with people.

◆ Try speaking to a stranger or performing an act of random kindness.

◆ Practise focusing your mind like a laser, perhaps concentrating on the word 'success' or 'joy' or 'power'.

◆ Try visualising a beautiful flower or a smiling face.

If you have any difficulty in some of these activities it may be that your body is too tense or your mind is holding too much turbulent energy. Find ways to relax and release any tension, such as taking a shower or doing some yoga or tai chi. Avoid anything that tends to disturb the mind, like being too busy or watching violent TV programmes.

## The Sacred Marriage

> *When opposites no longer damage one another,*
> *Both are benefited through attainment of Tao.*
> Tao Te Ching

The Warrior and Priestess face each other along the shoreline of subjective and objective reality. She sits in deep meditation, her face turned towards the light of the soul, feeling its gentle call. He stands poised in his chariot awaiting the signal to set the wheels in motion towards the next goal.

In my own life I have found it essential to engage with both sides of my conscious mind. For example I cycle to work each day through central London and in order to get there as efficiently and safely as possible I first register my intention of reaching my destination as quickly as possible and then I set off and open to the guiding touch of the Priestess. Through my body and feelings I usually get an immediate sense of safety or a warning to be cautious. Many times I have had advance warning when someone is about to do something unexpected. The Warrior part of me then knows how to take immediate action and will either slow down or make some avoiding manoeuvre.

When either the Warrior or the Priestess has been banished, the remaining side takes on the entire workload and there may be a sense of imbalance, with the danger of burn-out or depression ever present.

If the Priestess is overwhelmed or the Warrior collapses from nervous exhaustion, the conscious mind switches to 'automatic' and develops a negative ego or false self. However, when both aspects work together and co-operate the full energy of the conscious mind can be engaged and harnessed for the greater will of the soul and spirit.

By working to understand and bring into balance both sides of the conscious mind a greater awareness is naturally born. Awareness is the observer and director of our consciousness, which is the true place of authority within the conscious mind.

## Meditation on Inner Harmony (1)

*Once again close your eyes and begin to be aware of your breath, allowing any tension to flow out of you on the out-breath and drawing a golden white light into your lungs on the in-breath.*

*Continue until you feel your whole body is filled with this light, then bathe in the innocence and power of your being in this light. Allow this light to intensify slightly in your head and be absorbed by your brain.*

*Starting from the most dominant side of your brain, begin to build a bridge of light to the opposite side. If you have a strong Warrior side then begin to send a golden light from your left brain to your right brain. Do this by drawing light into the left hemisphere of your brain on the in-breath and on the out-breath imagine it flowing across to the right side. When you have connected the two sides in this way, begin with the opposite side and breathe white light into the right side, and then on the out-breath send this light to the left.*

*(If your Priestess side is stronger, begin by sending light from the right side to the left.)*

*Send strands of light between the two sides and visualise them being woven together. Continue until you have a sense that the task is done and then spend some time enjoying this feeling of connection. When you are ready slowly return to full waking consciousness, feeling this light with you for the rest of the day.*

## A Meditation on Inner Harmony (2)

*Once again sit in meditation and become aware of the breath and find your way to becoming still and relaxed. Breathe in light until you feel you are encased in an egg of light, and then imagine stepping through this light and out into an inner landscape. Trust the imagery that arises and find yourself again in nature. Open your inner senses and begin to look for a sacred place where you can meet your Warrior and Priestess. In this sacred place – which can be a grove of trees, a circle of stones or a crystal temple – mentally call to the Priestess to join you. Watch her approach and once again notice her appearance and allow her to draw near. Allow her to speak to you – she may communicate through words, feelings or physical sensations.*

*Then mentally call to the Warrior to join you and wait for him to come. See him draw near and once again notice his appearance. Open your heart to him and listen to any message he may have – he too may communicate through words, feelings or physical sensations. Then feel them both together and notice how they relate to each other. Are they friendly, indifferent or downright hostile? Then ask each one to merge their energies with yours and wait for each of them to step into you. When you have merged with both energies ask that they begin to harmonise within you. As you come back to waking consciousness know that you are bringing them both with you into the world.*

# 3 CHARTING INNER SPACE

*Before we can become fully divine,*
*we must become fully human.*

St Ignatius

## The Three Selves

We have taken a look at the power of the conscious mind, yet according to the Hawaiian shamanic wisdom of Huna, this is just one aspect of who we are. This ancient tradition states that there are at least three layers of consciousness or spirits that make up our psyche. These spirits or selves co-exist and magically co-create our individual reality, and they can and often do work wonderfully well together. When this happens life can blossom quite joyfully, yet when this is not the case and some form of internal disconnection or conflict occurs, life can become quite problematic or even painful.

### The Conscious Self

The first self, the Conscious Self, is affectionately known in various circles as the Talking Self or the Solar Self. This self begins to emerge during childhood, develops during adolescence, and starts to mature during the adult years. According to Erik Erikson, a leading figure in psychoanalysis and human development, the basis of developing a healthy ego or conscious mind depends on the quality of care received from parents or guardians. Where all of the survival needs of a child have been met, the foundation is laid for a positive and confident Conscious Self. However, where the developing consciousness has been exposed to strong ongoing criticism – or an environment of rejection, trauma, deep shame, despair or self-doubt

– the child's natural growth is likely to be inhibited. The Conscious Self is housed in the two hemispheres of the neo-cortex portion of the brain, as discussed earlier. On the one hand it is rational, logical, wilful and discerning, and on the other it is imaginative, feeling and intuitive. The Conscious Self has the power of speech and action, which it can use effectively, especially if both sides are working in harmony. It tends to waste precious energy when it loses touch with the present moment and becomes overly focused on thoughts of the past or fantasies of the future. This self knows how to distinguish between subjective and objective realities and, being a social self, is eager to relate and can grasp and appreciate other people's views on reality. This self asks 'Who am I?', 'What do I want?', 'What value is there in what I am doing?', 'Where am I going?' According to Huna wisdom this self is centred in the head and has the ability to separate from the physical body and to astral travel, either in meditation or in the dream state.

## *The Basic Self*

The next self roughly translates as the subconscious and unconscious minds of Western psychology, and is known as the Basic Self, or Lower Self in Huna. This self is also known in many circles as the Younger Self, the Inner Child or the Luna Self, and according to Huna and some other magical traditions it is considered to have many more abilities than is presently acknowledged by modern-day psychology. This self awakens in the womb as we begin our journey in the physical plane. Here it receives a download of genetic material from our parents, giving it the necessary instructions so it can begin to construct its physical vehicle. At birth the Basic Self is fully conversant with the emotional and mental environments it finds itself immersed in, and this information provides the entering soul with the co-ordinates that help it to anchor and orientate into its new circumstances. Through its DNA the Basic Self is able to access its ancestral inheritance and find much valuable information on how challenges were handled, successfully or otherwise, by past generations.

This self is the elemental portion of our consciousness that oversees, throughout our life journey, the building and regeneration of the body and all its involuntary bodily functions such as breathing, digestion and the pumping of the heart. It similarly regulates the flow of life-force energy (otherwise known as prana, mana, chi or ki) through the chakra system and various channels within the etheric energy body in order to vitalise the denser physical body.

This self is the Inner Child – the mute emotional self, the part of us that can laugh, smile, cry or scream. It does not communicate its needs through words but through feelings, physical sensations and the language of imagery and metaphor. It can, and often will, grab the attention of its sibling, the Conscious Self, through, for example, 'butterflies in the stomach'. When a stronger communication is needed, the body can be incapacitated in a number of ways, such as by catching a cold or getting a headache.

The Basic Self is our sexual self; we are all naturally sexual beings bursting with life-force energy, but this self can be conditioned to suppress this energy if need be. It is the holder of our ever unfolding sense of self and it builds a self-image from the messages it receives from its guardian figures – the family and the culture it finds itself within. It is the librarian that files away and acts on all the beliefs that are impressed upon it. These beliefs are fixed ideas about the world, and they act as instructions to the Basic Self covering everything it does, at either a physical or emotional level. It is important to note that many of these beliefs may be completely unknown or forgotten at a conscious level. Our Child Self contains the amazing ability to remember everything we have experienced in both this and previous lifetimes, and it is through this ability of memory that we are able to develop skills and accept both helpful and unhelpful conditioning. This ability to learn occurs through repetition, for the Basic Self is a slow but thorough learner. It can store memories of subjective events such as a dream and an external event such as going for a walk in the park. It does not make any distinction between either state and so a dream or a visualisation can have as great an impact as any actual physical event. The important factor is the intensity of the experience. This is an important point to note since it means that working with the imagination can lead to inner change. I once saw a very powerful documentary film on sharks that so worried my Child Self that it point blankly refused to allow me to go swimming in the sea off the south coast of England for weeks even though I knew logically that it was highly unlikely that I would encounter any sharks there. Every time I went to step in the water I had strong and fearful images of sharks arising from the deep to carry me off for their lunch.

The Basic Self is motivated by pleasure and pain, and it needs a sense of security and safety in the world if we are to function well. Without this fundamental sense of safety the Conscious Self will always be on shaky ground and consequently it will be very difficult for us to, say, meditate or engage meaningfully in any kind of spiritual practice. Because the Basic Self responds to love, doing something as simple as hugging a teddy bear or receiving an embrace goes a long way in convincing this Child Self that it is loved and is safe. As any mother knows, when a child is hurt a healing kiss does more to banish the pain than any lecture on good safety practice.

Like Rudyard Kipling's Mowgli the jungle boy, this self loves to be in nature and has a natural connection to all the spirits found in the kingdoms of nature. The Basic Self is the telepathic part of our consciousness that is able to communicate with other beings, human or otherwise, in ways beyond the abilities of the Conscious Self. Our Inner Child Self is naturally very spontaneous and loves to play.

Occasions like Christmas can evoke great wonder and joy within the Inner Child; its attention is readily grabbed by brightly decorated trees and enticingly wrapped gifts. This self can look out over a snow-covered landscape and simply be mesmerised by the magic of it all – and certainly has no problem in accepting that Father Christmas is able to deliver presents to all the children of the world in one night. Although our Inner Child is naturally magical, if it feels ignored and unloved its magic will begin to fade and dwindle. However, with time, love and patience that magic can be rekindled and burst into life once more.

The role of the Basic Self is to support the Conscious Self, rather like a servant. In a sense it is like a computer that can be programmed, or an animal that can be trained. The Basic Self is centred in the solar plexus region, and it stays in the physical body while the Conscious Self separates off when we are asleep or journeying in meditation.

## *A Journey to Meet the Basic Self*

*Find a comfortable position and begin to be aware of the cycle of your breath. Imagine that you can breathe light into the body and that you can feel this light rippling through you, rather like a stone dropped into a pond. As this light flows through the physical body you will feel very relaxed. As it flows into the emotions it has a wonderfully calming effect. As it flows into the mind it can smooth out and slow down the speed of your thinking processes.*

*In time allow this light to flow around your body and form a protective egg around it.*

*Eventually this egg may feel so full that the light will begin to change its nature and turn into a silvery white mist. This mist lovingly envelops and holds you, and you may feel it calls you to leave the mundane world and turn to the magical inner world.*

*Imagine stepping through this mist and eventually emerging into a landscape in nature. Use all your inner senses to feel, smell, see, listen to and taste this place. Feel your feet on the ground and see the colour of the sky above. This landscape is a unique place for you to explore. Somewhere in this landscape is a place with a spiral staircase descending into the earth. This staircase may be found in a hollow tree, a cave or a chasm in the ground. Find this place and stand before the staircase.*

*When you are ready, begin to descend. Do not worry about the dark since you will find that there is a pale light illuminating the way.*

*At the bottom of the stairs you may find a corridor and at the end of the corridor you may find a door. If so, walk along the corridor and stand before the door. Behind this door is a landscape where you will meet your Basic Self.*

*Open the door, pass through and close the door behind you. Stand for a while and allow the landscape to present itself to you. Do not attempt to imagine it; rather, allow it to present itself to your inner vision. However this place looks, whether inviting or not, step into it and begin to explore. Somewhere in this landscape is a building, which may be anything from a cottage to a palace. Trust that you know how to find this place and proceed through the landscape until you see a building in the distance. As you approach, notice how it looks and feels. Around the building is a garden, and it is here that you will meet your Basic Self. Mentally call for your Basic Self to join you, and then just wait for it to come and meet you. It may appear as a childlike figure, perhaps a younger version of you, or, more rarely, an animal. Allow it to appear however it wishes and sit and connect with this part of you. Does it feel shy and distrustful or very open? Tell your Basic Self that you wish to build a wonderful relationship with it and that you want its help in your life. Ask if there is anything it wants to tell you, and then just listen. It is important to spend some time simply listening and being open to its communication. Ask for a name which you can know it by from now on, and listen for it. Do not worry if you do not get one; in time you may. When the time seems right, and without rushing, begin to express as much love as you can to your Basic Self. Communicate your desire to be helpful and to assist in any healing that your Inner Child needs. Ask if there is anything it wishes you to do in the world. Your Basic Self may want you to be a little less serious and have more fun, or it may want you to climb trees or to paint or draw or write. Simply listen and decide later what you can commit to doing. You may not agree to do everything your Basic Self wants but you may choose to include some of the things in your life.*

*Hug and embrace this self if it will allow you to do so and, if you wish to, make a commitment to meet your Basic Self regularly. This will help develop trust in the relationship and deepen it.*

*Say farewell to your Basic Self and return to full waking consciousness by retracing your steps to the door by which you entered the landscape. Go through and close the door behind you, then ascend the steps to return to your body.*

## The Higher Self

The last self is generally known as the Higher Self. This does not mean that it is separate or more superior to the other two; rather, it simply exists in a different dimension. This self has also been called the Deep Self, the Divine Self, the Guardian Angel or the Stellar Self. This self is more mysterious since it exists beyond our everyday experience of time, space, form and polarity; however, this self is fully available and willing to become engaged in our everyday lives. In some ways it is like a personal guardian spirit that hovers above and beyond our Conscious Self, seeking to guide it. This self knows the reasons for our incarnation and has a grand overview of our life's path. As such it is constantly available for help, assistance, guidance and healing. It can inspire us through dreams or sudden intuitive flashes, and it uses synchronicity to reach out and touch us. It can communicate readily with Basic Self and, if the way is open, also with Conscious Self.

The home of the Higher Self is within multidimensional realms of pure consciousness, and therefore this self experiences time not as linear (as does the Conscious Self) but as simultaneous, for it walks within multifaceted realms of probability. This self is the highest potential that we seek and its abilities to help us in life cannot be overestimated. This self loves us unconditionally and it is the gateway through which every desirable soul quality or archetypal energy imaginable can flow. The Higher Self does not sit in judgement of the other two selves; it does not plan or direct their fate since that would interfere with the free will of the Conscious Self. However, once the Conscious Self has committed to a course of action (as long as this does not run counter to our chosen direction of growth) then the Higher Self will assist in every way conceivable. Our Higher Self exists within the great web of consciousness and is connected to every other Higher Self – and that includes the Higher Self of a group, a nation, and the whole of humanity. The Higher Self of humanity has also been called the Cosmic Christ or Buddha Consciousness.

## The Story of the Golden Buddha

*Long ago in a distant land there was a great Buddha statue made of pure gold that was as high as ten people. The Buddha statue sat in the lotus position in the tranquil garden of a monastery, and many people came to sit at its feet to pray or meditate.*

*Yet times were difficult and a great marauding army was at the borders of* the country and the community were unsure what to do. They feared for the safety of their beloved statue. Then one monk had the idea to disguise the statue so that it looked like ordinary stone. The monks and local people worked through the night to cover the statue with cement. When dawn broke the statue was completely covered.

Shortly afterwards the invading army arrived and as the soldiers passed by the statue they paid it no attention. The army stayed around the monastery for many years and by the time the army left no one in the village knew the true nature of the great Buddha statue.

One day a young man went to meditate against the Buddha and to his surprise a piece of the cement fell, revealing the gold underneath. Soon the local people were alerted and many came to help uncover the golden Buddha and restore it to its original beauty.

This true story is a great metaphor for consciousness and how at core we are all like the Golden Buddha. To this day the statue sits in the Temple of the Golden Buddha in Bangkok.

## Awakening the Light of the Higher Self

Find some time to be alone and to go within. Breathe into your body and imagine that you are absorbing a golden/white light into your lungs. Allow this light to fill your chest and on the out-breath let this light ripple throughout your body. In time imagine that your spine is filling with this light and that eventually this light extends simultaneously down into the earth and up through the top of your head towards the heavens. This light opens a channel that begins to connect you to Heaven and Earth.

Down this channel descends a radiant ball of light towards the top of your head. Allow this ball of light to enter through the crown of your head and fill your head and face with light. This light begins to dissolve any habitual personality masks that you wear and replaces it with a new lightness. This light can enter and fill your brain with radiant light and remove any blocks to your highest vision. This ball of light in time descends down towards your throat, where it opens your ability to express and communicate your wants and needs with grace. Simply allow any blocks to self-expression to melt away.

This ball of light then descends to your heart, where it begins to radiate unconditional love to your heart centre and melts away any heartbreak and barriers to intimacy. The ball of light descends further to the solar plexus, where it begins to dissolve all patterns of power struggle and replaces them with new patterns of co-operation and peace. It then descends to the area just below the navel, where it begins to radiate light to all old patterns of pain and suffering and replaces them with the light of joy.

The ball of light descends to the base of spine where it radiates the light of nurturing, dissolving any old patterns of fear and insecurity.

From here allow the ball of light to be absorbed into the very core of your body, into your very bones – which may begin to shine with diamond brilliance.

Now your Higher Self is absorbed into your physical, emotional and mental existence and its light will always be with you.

## Problems of Disharmony

The Basic Self is there as we enter life within the womb; it is there before we gradually develop a conscious mind. If its needs and wants are not met early on in life, patterns will develop in direct proportion and restrict its ability to trust other people. As infants we are vulnerable in the world and dependent on others for our very survival. During this time we may feel compelled to adopt certain ways of behaving in order to cope within our families. I can still remember being told when I was very young that 'children should be seen and not heard'. Similarly, many people grow up feeling they have never truly been listened to or seen within their families. This can lead to a sense of feeling bad or flawed in some way. Thus patterns of self-hatred can be set up when we are young. Without a basic sense of love, safety and security in the world, the emerging Conscious Self will not have a firm base from which it can be effective in life. Consequently much of its energy will be spent on continuously attempting to meet the insatiable needs of its sibling self.

The emerging Conscious Self may not have any appreciation that such a sibling self exists and may embark on a course of action that will distress that Child Self. Most problems of disharmony occur because of the way in which the Basic Self has been conditioned, and because of its later treatment at the hands of the Conscious Self. The Basic Self needs love, yet so often it is ignored or repressed rather than loved and cherished. Although we are loved unconditionally by our Higher Self, so often we are not conscious of that love and can feel alienated and alone and are thus more susceptible to developing attitudes and patterns that are critical and destructive.

Like any child the Basic Self needs love and acceptance from its older sibling self, and if this is not received it has a tendency to hide, create obstructions and cause difficulty. The Conscious Self is supposed to be the guardian of the Basic Self, but when that responsibility is not understood or it is disregarded the Basic Self has good reason to distrust and rebel against its guardian. The Priestess aspect of the Conscious Self can communicate with the Child Self and the Warrior provides a sense of protection. If one of these aspects is underdeveloped or missing, problems can occur. The Basic Self may reach a stage where it so distrusts the Conscious Self that it begins to look for guidance outside of the self, and that is never a healthy state of affairs.

The Basic Self cannot distinguish between the subjective and objective worlds and so can become greatly agitated if the Conscious Self continually focuses on fearful mental images. This causes the Basic Self to react as if it is under threat and activates the body's 'fight or flight' response, thus flooding the system with adrenaline to cope with the perceived danger. Where a Conscious Self tries to clamp down and repress certain thoughts and feelings, these can in time turn quite toxic. This may lead the Conscious Self to adopt further repressive approaches (addiction, distraction and denial, for example) to deal with this internal pain, and then it is heading for real difficulties. When the Basic Self is suppressed it is like a lid has been put on our life-force energy, sealing out both the pain and all our passion and emotional joy. The Basic Self contains our spontaneity, desire and enthusiasm – essential in helping us to live life to the full and to realise our dreams.

If the Conscious Self suppresses the natural physical and emotional impulses of the Basic Self, its own link to spirit is in danger of being distorted and even severed. When this happens the Conscious Self can become quite neurotic, seeing the universe as a hostile place where it needs to develop protective coping strategies in order to survive. Such a state heralds the birth of an adaptive negative ego or False Self, which represents an attempt by the Conscious Self to go on automatic pilot. The development of a False Self has now reached epidemic proportions in our world. Far from being a solution to the problem of a beleaguered Conscious Self, the False Self has itself become a far bigger problem. We will take a deeper look at this self a little later on.

The Inner Child does not have the resources to take over the role that is rightfully that of the Conscious Self for it cannot make adult choices. If the Conscious Self decides to abdicate its role as the director of its life and instead goes on automatic pilot and refuses to take responsibility, the Inner Child will feel abandoned and frightened. It may seek to grab the attention of its sibling through strong emotional or physical sensations, and if that does not work it may try stronger methods, perhaps through illness or accidents.

## Engaging the Basic Self in Magic

Working with energy and thereby creating magic is the natural province of the Basic Self, and so enchanting the Basic Self into co-operating in any magical or healing enterprise is a key step. Shamans and witches have known this for thousands of years and have sought the help of the Basic Self for bending and shaping reality. There are many methods that can be used, from rhythmic drumming, ecstatic dancing, hypnotic-sounding chanting, the lighting of candles, the use of impressive looking props such as crystal wands and special clothing, to the incantation of mystical poetry. Once the Basic Self is sufficiently engaged, motivated and then given clear instructions, it is easily able to perform miracles. What to the Conscious Self is a miracle, is to the Basic Self a natural event. Thus anything is possible to the Basic Self. We are now stepping into areas of belief, and belief is linked to faith. Faith has long been known to be a powerful factor in many areas, such as healing, and this is why the placebo effect occurs. Faith in this case is nothing more than the Basic Self being convinced that it should open to the healing power of the Higher Self and the unseen friends.

It is important to note that all the belief systems implanted or accepted into the Basic Self form the fundamental instructions with which the Basic Self creates reality. These instructions hold varying degrees of strength, which can be bypassed temporarily by magical acts such as rituals and spells. The effect is permanent only if the beliefs themselves are altered, otherwise the force behind the beliefs snaps back into place after a while and restores reality to its familiar state. We will be exploring this in more depth very shortly.

The Basic Self is very connected to the spirit world and that is why children, who are not usually so hindered by doubts and fears, can see spirits more easily than many adults. This ability unfortunately disappears if the message gets across that such visions are nothing more than pure fantasy, or perhaps even dangerous. When this happens the Basic Self dutifully switches off any psychic abilities and does not restore them until it is again convinced that there is nothing wrong with such innate tendencies.

The Basic Self is affected by the phases of the moon and in lesser degrees by the movement of the planets within the solar system. The moon, being the closest heavenly body to the earth, has a strong effect on the physical body and the emotional field and that is why it is considered important in magical circles to align any act of magic or manifestation to the appropriate phase of the moon.

The conscious mind can learn to reprogramme some of the instructions held in the Basic Self and thus begin to transform every sphere of life – improving the overall sense of wellbeing, making more energy available, clearing obstacles to earning money – in ways that feel joyful and useful. Similarly, less useful conditioning – being closed to telepathic communication or the clamping down of sexual energy – can be replaced with more liberating instructions.

## Reprogramming the Basic Self

+ Use to your advantage the fact that the Basic Self is impressionable and can be conditioned.

+ Be aware of the data coming in through your senses and as far as possible adjust your environment to make it as pleasant as possible.

+ Use uplifting imagery and symbolism to energise, inspire and nurture your Basic Self.

+ Practise sending to your Basic Self positive mental commands throughout the day, such as 'I release now all internal confusion' or 'I am living in an abundant and loving universe'. Listen to the response of your Basic Self; if it presents you with old painful memories or fearful feelings simply imagine these being burnt or torn up and thrown in a waste bin. Through continuing to reaffirm positive thoughts and commands and sending out messages to remove old fearful thoughts and feelings, your new instructions will in time take root.

• Say out loud uplifting affirmations as you take physical exercise such as walking or cycling. Speaking in time to any physical action helps them to take root faster.

• Use visualisation to change any negative scripts you hold – such as 'I am a loser' or 'nothing ever works out for me' – to positive ones where you are a 'winner' or a 'success'.

• Visualise new scenarios and play at being a hero or a magician, overcoming many challenges to achieve your goals. Practise learning to see yourself being able to overcome any challenge to obtain your heart's desire – and, above all, be creative. Think of yourself as an artist, and the Basic Self as the canvas or clay with which you create.

Enjoy the process of reprogramming your Basic Self.


## Becoming the Guardian of the Basic Self

> *If you follow the Huna precepts of loving yourself [Basic Self] first, putting it before all others in importance, defending it from others and never rejecting or insulting it, you will find its naturally trusting nature emerging. Communication will become free and honest.*
> Enid Hoffman

In my own life I have found that once I consciously commit to stepping on a path of growth and awakening, the first thing I need to do – and quite rapidly – is to expand the horizons of my Conscious Self and in a sense re-educate myself. This has helped me to clarify what was holding me back in life so that I can get to work stretching those boundaries. The next stage is to re-parent my Basic Self and begin to transform the limiting conditioning that makes me feel unworthy, undeserving, unloved and disconnected. This in turn leads me to feeling more connected to spirit, and as a result my intuition feels crisper and more accurate and my effectiveness in the world begins to increase.

The basic principle to remember when working with our different selves is that it is the job of the Conscious Self to love and take care of the Basic Self. This opens the way for the Higher Self to love and take care of the Conscious Self, since most of the barriers to connection with spirit exist within the Basic Self. As the Conscious Self embraces the Basic Self, the path that allows the love of the Higher Self to flow through is cleared. By working to embrace the Child Self we can free its immense emotional warmth, intimacy, innate sense of magic, wonder and playfulness, and at the same time open ourselves to the light of the Higher Self. Through working to clear away the hurts of the past and by accepting and forgiving all the 'stuff' we are holding within the Basic Self, we begin to heal any sense of internal disconnection and alienation.

It is important to be aware that every thought, word and action carried out by the Conscious Self has an impact on the Basic Self and conditions it into creating programmes that attract experience, either joyful or painful, for the future. Knowing this, an aware Conscious Self can change its habitual way of thinking, speaking and acting in the world and begin to practise sending comforting thoughts to the Basic Self, especially when it signals that it is frightened. Thoughts such as 'I love and care for you' and 'do not worry, all is well' can work at one level. Saying aloud a reassuring statement can work at another level, and taking a nurturing action (such as having a warm bath with beautiful music and candlelight) works at yet another.

The imagination is a powerful tool; use it to send comforting images to the Basic Self (by visualising your Inner Child being hugged by someone loving), or to imagine your Inner Child receiving the safety it needs (being in a warm room surrounded by things it loves) or to see yourself taking the child somewhere nice (such as the seaside or a funfair). Relaxation and conscious deep breathing can help immensely in connecting the Conscious and Basic selves.

The Basic Self is highly suggestible, as any good hypnotist or practitioner in Neuro-Linguistic Programming knows. It can thus be reprogrammed by the Conscious Self through creative visualisation, ritual, intention, positive thought, word (spoken and written), action and new choices. Frequent repetition of written and spoken affirmations helps in the reprogramming, for the Basic Self is a slow learner. In its role as guardian the Conscious Self can devise more joyful and life-affirming rituals for the child-like self. A ritual can be as simple as lighting a candle with intention, wearing a piece of jewellery that has a symbolic meaning attached to it by the Conscious Self, or watching a video that will appeal to your Inner Child.

The Basic Self is the emotional self, but without the detachment and insight that the Conscious Self brings there is always the danger of being flooded and paralysed with emotion. Emotions are wonderful and are what make us fully human, yet if they are constantly running in response to some long-past yet unresolved trauma we can never really live in the present moment.

Imagine for a moment that your Basic Self is like a dog that you love deeply. This dog is very playful and spontaneous and has a strong instinct. It seeks to exist with the least possible pain and resistance, unless motivated otherwise by you. You may teach it some basic tricks, such as learning to fetch a ball, which it masters after some effort on your part. It comes to respect your authority and you know not to be cruel (because if you are your pet may dare to bite the hand that feeds it). Although this dog may have been conditioned to react to other people in either a frightened or aggressive manner, you realise that this can be overcome through kindness and firmness.

## Being a Guardian

Things to avoid:

◆ People who are aggressive or critical towards your Child Self.

◆ Speaking to others in ways likely to disturb your Child Self, such as in an aggressive or judgemental manner.

◆ Frightening your Basic Self with violent stories or images via the media.

◆ Eating or drinking anything that your body finds over-stimulating or difficult to digest.

Things to do:

◆ Listen to soothing music or beautiful poetry.

◆ Find ways to create space for inner stillness, such as attuning to the stillness in nature.

◆ Create a space for relaxation and release any tension you are holding in the body, perhaps through massage, dancing, bodywork or forms of exercise such as yoga or tai chi.

◆ Begin to practise meditation every day to evoke calmness and relaxation in the conscious mind. Find time for your Inner Child in meditation, to strengthen your connection. Speak to this self as if it were with you all the time (which it actually is) and reassure it that you do care and love it and will protect it from harm. Commit to taking care of your vulnerability and protecting it from harm, shame or pain.

◆ Take care of yourself by getting enough sleep, eating a balanced and healthy diet and drinking plenty of pure water

◆ Before speaking and acting spend a moment considering whether it will enhance or diminish your sense of inner harmony.

◆ Learn to face difficult feelings that you may have been suppressing, perhaps through counselling or by talking to people you can trust.

Things to check out:

◆ Look to your choices and see which ones are helpful in bringing about inner harmony and which ones create discord. Look at your choices around boundaries, protecting your vulnerability and owning your power. Look at how much you criticise and attack yourself for not being clever, beautiful, spiritual or successful enough. Find strategies for creating more self-love and nurturing in your life.

◆ Ask yourself which things, situations or people give you a sense of an increased level of energy and which give you a sense of heaviness and decreased level of energy. (These are messages from the Basic Self about what makes it happy.)

◆ Check whether you are expressing your sexual energy in a way that increases your self-love or your self-hatred. Are you in touch with your inner feminine or masculine nature?

## Overcoming Inner Confusion

*A great way to clear inner confusion is to say 'yes' only to those things you want to engage with in life and 'no' to those things you do not wish to engage with.*

*The Basic Self is very confused when we say 'yes' to a course of action and start committing to things we do not want. This sets up a programme within the Basic Self's mindset, one that says, 'When I say "yes" I really mean "no"', or vice versa.*

*What do you want to say 'yes' to in your life? What do you want to say 'no' to in your life?*

*Make it a daily practice to speak only from the heart and to commit only when your heart says 'yes' to something. (This does not mean that you can never change your mind, only that this should be the exception rather than the norm.)*

*Following on from this is the need to make clear agreements with other people. Clear agreements help to avoid misunderstanding and lay a good foundation for committing to a path of action.*

# 4 TEMPLES OF BELIEF

*People are disturbed not by things,*
*but by the view they take of them.*

Epictetus

## Why Are Beliefs Important?

The Conscious Self with all its abilities is the programmer of our reality and the Basic Self is the mechanism or hardware that accepts instructions and goes about generating our experience of reality. Beliefs form the foundation of who we think we are and are an integral part of our identity and self-image. A belief is a thought that has somehow become frozen at some point in our lives and turned into a universal truth. Beliefs are the invisible software that generates our moment-to-moment experience of reality, and it is a part of the human experience to adopt beliefs. In this world of more than five billion souls there are an equal number of unique ways of interpreting reality since everyone has the capacity of choice and no one is born into exactly the same set of circumstances. Even where large groups of people subscribe to similar beliefs – such as members of a religious group or a political party – no two people will agree exactly on how life works, or act in the world in the same way. Beliefs naturally vary in strength, depending on the importance placed on them, and so at one end of the scale they can be an absolute certainty that something is right or true and at the other end more like an inclination towards accepting that something is right or true. Beliefs are nothing more than a current understanding of how life works based on attitudes and experience, although they are often felt to be a hotline to 'the truth'. Beliefs can be based on objective facts, but always there is some element of opinion mixed in. Time and time again the world of politics has shown how statistics can be packaged to give different versions of the truth. In a sense this book is another example since I am writing from my own current level of understanding and so am naturally inclined to present information and talk about experiences that are in line with my beliefs. This has been an important point for me to bear in mind: I have come across many different teachers, both in the spirit world and the outer physical world, and I have realised that all of them can teach only from the place they have reached in their own spiritual journey and so can take students only so far. Similarly, a certain belief can be liberating for a time and then become a barrier that must be passed. Beliefs are thus the stepping-stones to liberation or enlightenment – and also the stones with which we construct our own prisons.

Our beliefs span every area of life – from health, love, money, relationships and spirituality to synchronicity. Some people see and experience life as a struggle, for others it is a wonderful journey. Some believe and experience money to be a scarce commodity, others see and experience the world as an abundant place where all their needs and wants are met. Some people believe and experience people to be fundamentally 'good' and helpful, others see and experience them as cold and cruel. Which version is true? Only you can decide. Because strong convictions have some sort of impact on our lives it is immensely helpful to discover which ones work in our favour and which ones bind us. Core beliefs tend to be held in place with a lot of emotional force, and that is why when one of them is challenged it can provoke a very angry and defensive outburst. You may have experienced an occasion when someone dared to question one of your beliefs about life and you reacted angrily or fearfully. I still remember an 'appreciation' exercise that I took part in on a team-building day-workshop I attended a number of years ago. In turn, each member of the team had to sit in the middle of the group for three or four minutes and silently receive positive feedback from the others. I vividly remember my inner agony because I then had beliefs that said I was not really worthy of any praise. I remember hearing some of these comments and inwardly dismissing then as untrue or simply flattery. These comments challenged how I saw myself at the time and so I did my utmost to shut them out.

## How We Accept Beliefs

We accept beliefs from the time we are growing in the womb until the time we depart this world. Our beliefs at five years of age will no doubt be different from the ones we live with in adulthood – if they are not we are either an enlightened soul or heading for trouble. Every experience in life can potentially lead to the creation of a meaning about life or ourselves through the lens of that experience. This happens from very early on as the Basic Self, from within the womb, begins to orientate itself within the environment of the family's collective beliefs. As we grow up and form a conscious mind we can move beyond the sphere of the family and go out into the world and begin to re-evaluate those beliefs. This is why travel and contact with diverse cultures is so useful, for it allows ideas that have been taken for granted to be seen in a new light. Inevitably we are exposed to the belief systems that are dominant in our culture, and we therefore find ourselves in the midst of a whole range of conflicting beliefs about everything – from what it means to be a man or a woman, to ideas about wealth and social justice, and death. As we grow up our Basic Self accepts belief systems in order to make sense of reality. These beliefs can be positive and useful (such as 'You are very creative', 'You were born to be very successful', or 'You are so loved') or limiting (such as 'You will never amount to anything', 'What is the point in even trying?', 'There is something wrong with you'). Each one of us inevitably carries a unique set of beliefs that reflects the current stage of our journey through life, and all other lifetimes. Most of the time we are not totally aware of the beliefs being passed to us, especially within our family, because they are not always communicated directly. Verbal communication accounts for only a small percentage of the many ways in which human beings communicate: body language, facial expression, tone of voice, emotionally charged silences and telepathic communication are all capable of communicating beliefs. Family or peer pressure plays a part in our conditioning too.

One of my closest friends was brought up in a very orthodox Jewish family with strong expectations that she would marry and stay within the faith. Eventually she looked for and found inspiration in other spiritual paths and started to have relationships with men outside her faith. She became increasingly frightened that her family would find out and disown her, so hid an important part of her life from them for many years; this caused her considerable unhappiness. In time she managed to see how much her beliefs affected her choices in life and was able to make some changes. She now experiences a more joyful relationship with her family and feels happier in her friendships.

## How Our Beliefs Form Our Experience of Reality

Beliefs create our experiences at two levels. Level 1 operates in both our subjective and objectives worlds and may be the easier level to understand and appreciate since an inspirational idea followed through can change the course of our lives and an emotion thoughtlessly expressed can create an immediate reaction. Level 2 is more difficult to appreciate since it is entirely subjective and more intangible; however, its consequences can be seen in recurring patterns or streaks of 'good' or 'bad' luck.

## 1 *The Impact of Thought, Emotion, Choice, Expectation, Speech and Action*

Our beliefs determine the focus, quality and direction of our thoughts. We have so many thoughts each day and the process is often so automatic that we give little consideration to the 50,000 or so thoughts that may flicker across our awareness before passing on. This stream of mental energy can be like a fast-flowing crystal-clear river or a murky stream incapable of sustaining much life. We may think about losing our job or think that a wonderfully rewarding job may just be around the corner; we may ponder on asking an attractive person out for a date or think that such a proposition would end in a humiliating rejection. We may be preoccupied or obsessed with thoughts of sex, spirituality, shopping, relationships, money or career, depending on the nature of the beliefs that generate them. These thoughts cause us to feel certain emotions, which are either pleasant and expansive or unpleasant and contractile. We may feel elated or depressed, happy or sad, depending on the nature of our thinking.

Our emotions and thinking process affect the choices we make in the world, from the words we choose to utter to the actions we choose to take or refrain from. We make ongoing choices about everything, from the way we take care of our body, to the books we read and the people we are attracted to or repelled by. Some choices become so habitual that it seems like no choice is available at all. Each morning we get up and make a number of habitual decisions about life, such as whether or not we will be happy that day. We do not say or do anything unless we believe in it, and even when we are being dishonest and not speaking or acting from our deepest truth we do so only because we believe in the necessity and benefit of being deceitful.

Our beliefs give free range to our imagination and creative abilities or close them down. They affect our experience of wellness, determine our ability to be aware, influence how we feel about the future and the past and determine what we expect to happen to us throughout life. We expect success or failure, happiness or misery, support or neglect, or perhaps miracles or monotony. You may have noticed that you almost always get what you deep-down expected. You may even catch yourself saying 'That always happens to me!' Our beliefs grant free expression to certain thoughts and emotions whilst restricting others. For example, we may decide that grief is bad because we consider it weak to cry, or we may decide that no one ever listens to us, because we were never much listened to as a child, and so we need to make a big fuss to get certain needs met. Our beliefs affect the way we experience life through the five senses for they instruct the Basic Self to be on the lookout for certain things and to ignore others. For instance, if we live in a city we may well believe that cities are exciting places, alive and full of things to do, and the countryside is boring, smelly and unfriendly. If this is so, when we do visit the countryside we are literally programming our senses to be on the lookout for everything that is wrong with it – and will be only too happy to return to the buzz of the city as soon as possible.

All blocks in life originate from our beliefs and these manifest through our excuses, our hidden agendas and the stories we tell ourselves to explain away any misfortune or bad luck. The good news is that no belief is sacrosanct unless you say it is, and every limiting belief can be transformed if you say it can.

> *You form the fabric of your experience*
> *through your own beliefs and expectations.*
> Seth

## 2 Everything is Connected Through Vibration

This level works through the principle that everything is interconnected, including our inner subjective realm of consciousness and our outer reality. The relationship between inner and outer is one important aspect of polarity and it is a basic principle of magic and manifesting. When we understand this relationship we can consciously grip the reins of our lives instead of being unconsciously dragged along by forces beyond our control. This principle works because we are all connected at a deep level, and at the level of our superconscious self there is no such thing as separation. In the first three decades of the nineteenth century a number of paradoxical discoveries in the atomic and subatomic worlds opened up a debate in the scientific community. Some broke away from the general agreement that saw the universe as some great lifeless machine devoid of any guiding intelligence and instead took a more holistic view of the cosmos. These new discoveries changed the way science viewed physical matter, where solid and separate objects begin to dissolve into wave-like patterns of probabilities. According to the physicist Fritjof Capra, in his book *The Web of Life*, these patterns are probabilities of interconnectedness: 'subatomic particles have no meaning as isolated entities but can be understood only as interconnections'. Thus science itself is opening to a more mystical worldview that sees all life as part of a connecting and holistic system. Interconnectedness explains why prayer can touch and uplift another, how telepathy and intuition can work and how synchronicity is possible. Every counsellor knows the power of empathy and how it forms within the context of a relationship. You too may have felt stirrings of this at work at those times when you followed an irrational gut feeling and found it led to a perfect outcome, or when you instinctively knew when someone was angry, sad or unhappy even when they seemed fine on the outside. Everything in our universe is constantly in a state of vibration and motion, from the smallest atom to the grandest star, and we humans are no different. We broadcast on spiritual, mental, emotional and etheric bands and are like an orchestra that constantly plays to the cosmos. We attract or repel all experiences through this personal broadcast and so, for example, if we are looking for a sexual partner we send out a signal that attracts either the soul mate of our wildest dreams or the cellmate of our worst nightmares. The important factor that determines the quality of this broadcast is whether our beliefs are predominantly fear- or love-based – both are highly magnetic and both will create very different experiences. If you want to know the quality of your beliefs just take a look at your life and see if you are living a life that is a joy to behold or a living nightmare. Heaven and hell are states of consciousness before they manifest themselves to us. Reality is a feedback system where the quality of our thoughts, emotions and beliefs is reflected back to us. This process usually happens quite unconsciously within most people and the challenge is to make it as conscious as possible.

## A Look at Beliefs

> *Do not believe in what you have heard; do not believe in traditions because they have been handed down for many generations; do not believe in anything because it is rumoured and spoken of by many; do not believe merely because the written statements of some old sages are produced; do not believe in conjecture;*
>
> *do not believe in that as a truth to which you have become attached by habit;*
>
> *do not believe merely on the authority of your teachers and elders.*
>
> The Buddha

Two lists of beliefs follow: the first is more fear based and therefore may feel more contractile; the second is more love based and may feel more expansive. Take a long slow look at these and notice if any touch a chord inside of you. Notice which ones you agree with, which ones you have no opinion on, and which ones you feel are definitely untrue.

## Examples of Fear-Based Beliefs

*I am powerless and cannot cope.*

*I am at the mercy of my past conditioning.*

*My class or racial background determines my opportunities in life.*

*I am at the mercy of my fate, destiny or karma.*

*My future is bleak.*

*There is not enough money, resources, love or opportunities to go around.*

*People are basically selfish and out for themselves.*

*Life is full of suffering.*

*Suffering is good for the soul.*

*Life is meant to be a struggle.*

*The universe is a hostile place, and people are out to get me.*

*I am flawed and defective.*

*I was born in a state of sin and I deserve to be punished.*

*I am a worthless failure with no value whatsoever.*

*I cannot have what I want in life.*

*Happiness never lasts or always leads to disappointment.*

*Romantic love always hurts.*

*I am just not the sort of person that can be or have …*

*It always happens that way for me.*

*I cannot let go of … because …*

*I do not deserve.*

*Death is the end of my existence.*

## Examples of Love-Based Beliefs

*I am resourceful and can cope with whatever life brings my way.*

*I can transform my personality so that it is a helpful ally in my life.*

*My power is in the present moment.*

*I determine my life's path.*

*My parents did their best and offered me many gifts.*

*I can always do or have what I want.*

*Life is full of opportunities.*

*People are basically loving.*

*Life is filled with joy and wonder.*

*Joy is the natural state of my being.*

*The universe is a friendly and supportive place.*

*People are out to help me.*

*I am perfectly imperfect.*

*I was born in a state of grace.*

*I am a valuable person.*

*I am a success.*

*Happiness lasts and leads to fulfilment.*

*I deserve.*

*Love heals. I have an open and radiant heart.*

*I am the sort of person that can be or have ...*

*I am lucky.*

*I can easily let go of ... because ...*

*I grow wiser as I grow older.*

*I am inner directed and find much wisdom lies within me.*

*Death is the beginning of a new existence.*

## *An Example Of How Beliefs Can Affect Our Lives*

Sexuality is an emotive subject and has long been a fertile field for all sorts of ideas. Within Western society there are many limiting ideas in circulation about how this energy should be expressed. Religion in particular has had a lot to say in this area and over time in many ways it has succeeded in persuading people that sex and sin are linked. This has generated much fear and confusion, coupled with a considerable degree of control and suppression. Religion has tended to view the physical body and also physical life as inferior to the soul and the life hereafter. To add to the confusion, women have been idolised for their virginity and purity on the one hand and despised for their carnal nature on the other. The film industry has linked evil and sexuality in a number of horror/thriller movies. Often the saintly man is lured to his doom by the beautiful and lusting female vampire, though usually there is a happy ending and she is later slain by the good and courageous male vampire slayer. Patriarchal societies have tended to promote the idea that man is the hunter, woman the prize. Men who have many conquests are often highly regarded by their male peers, yet women who seduce men are often thought of in more derogatory terms – after all, look what happened after Adam was seduced by Eve! As long as sexuality is bound by such limiting ideas, how can we ever truly be free to find and express sexual intimacy with love? Our distant ancestors would not have understood such polarised views of sexuality – in Britain our Celtic ancestors granted women a far greater degree of sexual autonomy than is today regarded as normal or decent. How can our culture hold purity in high esteem and yet use the power of sexual attraction as a means to sell goods and services? Women's bodies in particular have been used in this way, and there has been a strong attempt throughout the ages to control and channel the sexuality of women.

There are many different ideas about what is a 'normal' or natural expression of sexual energy, and homosexual relationships have long suffered because of this. I am meeting more and more people who are interested in opening up to new possibilities in this area, who are becoming tired of antiquated ideas about how to live and love. Recently there has been an increase of interest in paths of sacred sexuality – such as Tantra and aspects of paganism – that seek to heal the artificial split between sexuality and spirituality so long encouraged by religion. These paths are very helpful, I have found, in both liberating the Basic Self from ideas of sin and guilt and allowing greater intimacy, play and joy so that sexual expression becomes a sacred meditation. When the Basic Self is liberated from limiting and fixed ideas on how sexuality should be expressed, we can truly find the magic of sex and see it as a path to touching the spirit.

## Some New Thoughts

*My body is the physical manifestation of my soul.*

*Sexual energy is Divine.*

*I am able to lovingly express my sexual desire.*

*I am free to choose how I express my sexual desire.*

*I am open to knowing both sexual pleasure and innocence.*

*My sexual energy is a key to knowing my creativity.*

*My sexual energy is a key to manifestation.*

*I feel safe in expressing who I am.*

*I love and honour the needs of my body.*

*I release all my guilt and shame around my sexuality.*

*I am open to meeting a loving partner who can fulfil all my wants and needs.*

## How to Find Our Beliefs

It is important to discover any limiting belief so that the process of transforming it into something more useful can begin. The Basic Self is usually happy to be of service and help you, although it may sometimes resist if it feels frightened about something. Like a frightened child it may seek to avoid certain things, and so lots of love and patience can be helpful. Some beliefs may be obvious, others may be deeply concealed. There are three ways to discover beliefs:

- Direct questioning
- Emotional surfing
- Mental surfing

The following exercises will take you through each one.

## Direct Questioning

Take a look at the questions below and allow yourself to answer them from both the head and the gut. Be aware of all the thoughts that are clamouring for attention and feel all of your emotions that the question evokes; censor nothing and allow both 'negative' and 'positive' responses to come up.

- What do I think is right and wrong about the world?

- What do I believe about … (choose a subject such as money, health, love or life)?

- What do I believe about people who have this thing (perhaps you see them as arrogant, smart, greedy or charismatic)?

- What do I believe is blocking me in life (such as my past, feeling I am not good enough or do not deserve anything, or a feeling of inner confusion)?

- What are my deepest fears?

- What do I believe about the future?

You may wish to add more questions to the list.

Take a look at what you have written and see if you can spot any of your beliefs. Highlight the helpful beliefs in one colour and the unhelpful ones in another.

## Emotional Surfing

When you feel emotional about something in your life use this exercise to get to the beliefs that lie at the core of the issue. The exercise requires a willingness to face any unpleasant feelings you may have, staying with them in order to ride them to the core beliefs that generated them.

Sit in silence and simply notice all the emotions flowing through you, making no attempt to suppress any of them. Become aware of your cycle of breath and allow all emotional energy to flow through you. Notice where you feel tense and consciously relax your body. Tune into your emotions and follow where they want to flow, see what images they evoke in your mind, experience what feelings they evoke in your body and listen to what they have to say. Allow them full expression and dive as deeply as you can. Although this may feel painful, awareness will lead to healing. Allow any tears or laughter to surface and continue to dive into the heart of your feelings. Like an explorer, seek to find the treasures your emotions contain and go deeper in search of the original trauma that is at the heart of the problem. Continue to allow everything to arise as you ride the emotion into the core of the issue and go on for as long as you can or until the emotional force begins to subside. This exercise can lead to a lot of release and it is important to let everything flow through you. Simply notice any memories, thoughts or feelings that come up and allow them to pass through you. Then allow everything to flow out of you; hold on to nothing. At the end of this exercise stand in nature with bare feet to allow any excess energy to drain away. Alternatively, place your hands on the earth and ground the energy that way.

Review your journey and take note of anything surprising that came up.

## Mental Surfing

*Find a comfortable posture and begin to be aware of your cycle of breath. Imagine you can breathe in light, and on the out-breath release all tension. Bring to mind an area where you want more clarity; get clear on what you want to know and then let the issue go. Turn inwards and begin to find yourself standing on the top of a spiral staircase that descends into the earth. Open your inner senses and see, feel, smell, hear and generally sense being in your inner world.*

*Begin to descend the staircase. When you arrive at the bottom you find yourself in a corridor. Walk along this corridor, noticing all that you can about it – its smell, its feel and how much light there is. When you come to the end you will find a door. Stand in front of the door and bring your chosen issue to mind once more. Behind the door will be a scene that will speak to you symbolically about your beliefs on that issue. When you are ready, step through the door and begin to explore what lies beyond.*

*Allow the images simply to show up, rather like turning on a TV, and avoid any desire to interfere with what your Basic Self wants to present to you. Just trust that the right images will come. At first you may receive impressions rather than clear visual images, and this is fine. Use all of your senses and allow the imagery to become crisper and clearer. Where are you? What can you see or feel? Imagine that you can reach out and touch something in your landscape, listen to the sounds and smell the smells. Do you feel*

> *expansive or contractile in this place? Explore this landscape and*
> *find out what lies there. Notice everything and gather as much*
> *information as you can. Notice the symbolic language of the*
> *subconscious as it speaks to you through metaphor and imagery.*
> *When you are ready to leave, retrace your steps and concentrate*
> *again on your breathing to bring you back to full waking*
> *consciousness.*

Write down all the symbols you encountered and how you felt about them. Understanding this journey is very much like trying to interpret a dream. Do not look for a self-help guide; simply ask yourself what these images mean to you. Give yourself lots of space to allow the answers to come.

## Changing Beliefs

> *Every truth passes through three stages*
> *before it is recognised.*
> *In the first, it is ridiculed.*
> *In the second, it is opposed.*
> *In the third it is regarded as self-evident.*
>
> Arthur Schopenhauer

Changing the beliefs that block us in life does not mean we must suddenly become naive or pretend that certain things no longer exist; rather, it is a process of expanding our point of view to a more liberating one. We might believe quite strongly that the world is a hostile and dangerous place and we may see or hear of many things that reinforce this viewpoint. We might find ourselves getting quite angry or afraid when we think about the way things are, or how in the future they might get worse. I feel I can speak with some expertise on this one since this was my conviction for many years. We all experience many things in life and we all create meaning from those experiences. Beliefs start to create reality at levels 1 and 2 and very soon there is plenty of evidence to support any strongly held belief. I once heard a story in a personal development seminar about two boys who were brought up by their alcoholic father; one went on to become an alcoholic and the other became a successful lawyer. They were each asked why they had turned out the way they had and they both replied: 'With a father like mine, what did you expect?'

The main challenge when working with beliefs is that we are not totally conscious of everything we believe. Only when a belief becomes conscious can it be held up to the light by the Conscious Self who must ask 'Is this belief of value?' If the answer is 'no' then regardless of whether it is considered right or wrong the belief needs to be transformed into a more liberating one. Now it may seem obvious that some things, such the daily rising and setting of the sun, will not change whatever the state of our beliefs, because such things are set in motion by a consciousness far beyond our present comprehension. There are certain laws, such as the law of gravity, that bind us into a collectively shared experience of life. Some masters and awakened souls have shown that many of these laws can be altered, and there are many reports of awakened beings performing miracles. I have a number of friends who have attended a fire-walking workshop and walked across hot coals without getting burnt. The method is always the same, to work on believing that it is possible. Many things are held to be an absolute truth on the basis of how many people believe them to be true. An examination of history will reveal that absolute truths have a habit of changing over time. At a personal level our opinions have a habit of solidifying into absolute truths. In order to be free and to know our innermost potential, all of these must be continually examined and where necessary changed. We will know when a belief has been changed because our life will change in some way.

## The Five Stages of Changing Beliefs

*In working with changing beliefs there are five stages.*

*1 Discovering the limiting belief.*

*2 Finding a new belief that is both beneficial and the exact opposite of the limiting one.*

*3 Working to open to the possibility of the new thought being true.*

*4 Beginning to believe in the probability of the new thought.*

*5 Developing a deep conviction in the new thought.*

Positive thinking alone can bring only temporary results; in addition the sponsoring beliefs behind 'negative' thinking need to be discovered and transformed. Otherwise, when the guard and focus of the Conscious Self is relaxed the beliefs behind negative thinking will re-emerge. Imagine your beliefs are a house. Some beliefs are like supporting walls that hold up the entire structure, others are like bricks or roof tiles and are easy to replace. Core belief structures are held in place by a lot of mental and emotional energy, and changing them will bring more dramatic change in the outer world. Of course many beliefs work positively in our lives and do not need changing. And these beliefs we can reinforce. Changing those beliefs that do not work so well is like calling in builders to repair and renovate your house so it becomes a more beautiful, expansive and pleasurable place to live in. Remember, we may have held some beliefs inside ourselves for many years or even lifetimes, and so some commitment and patience may be necessary to alter this habitual flow of mental and emotional energy.

Our Basic Self creates our experience of reality through the beliefs we hold. These are the baseline instructions that determine how we experience life, and the simple rule is that when we truly change a belief we will in time change our life. This change may not be immediate since there is usually a time factor involved. The force of an old belief may reverberate for a while into the future until its effect fades and the new belief begins to snap into place.

In my own life I believed for many years that work had to be a slog and had to be endured to earn enough money to survive. I also believed that I had little of what was needed to make a success of my life, and I rapidly developed an image of myself as a failure. It wasn't until I hit 40 that I realised that I held some very strong limiting beliefs in these areas and set about changing things. Despite a lot of inner work, things changed but slowly over a three-year period because of the power of my old beliefs in failure.

## How to Change Your Beliefs

1 Discover the nature of your limiting beliefs and ascertain how strongly you hold them to be true.

2 Feel how this view of reality is holding you back in life. Also, know that you can change this belief.

3 Choose an opposite, uplifting thought to supersede the old belief. Be very clear on the new thought. Make this thought indicate that it is something happening in the present moment rather than something that can happen in the future. Thoughts that begin 'I am' are the most useful.

4 Begin to work on focusing on the new thought so that it can take root as a belief.

5 Hold the new thought in your mind and remind yourself of this thought throughout the day. Choose a physical object to remind you of the new thought; this can be anything from an item of clothing to a piece of jewellery. Every time you see the object you will be reminded of the new thought.

6 Meditate on the new thought and feel the new expansive feeling that it brings. Allow the tone of this feeling to radiate throughout your whole being. (During this whole process it is likely that thoughts based on old beliefs will emerge to grab your attention. Each time you catch yourself thinking about an old belief imagine it being written out in your mind. Then find a way to cancel or destroy the words, perhaps by drawing a red line through them or seeing them burst into flames. Or perhaps visualise ripping up the belief as if it were a page in a book. Then imagine seeing the new thought being written out in your mind. Imagine filling it with light and placing the thought in a sacred place.)

7 Engage your emotions in the new thought and feel the excitement, joy and passion of having it manifest in your reality. Notice any emotional energy that wants to come up in support of your old worldview. Do not suppress these feelings; simply acknowledge their presence and return to empowering your new belief.

8 Make new choices that are in line with this new belief. If you want more love then start being and giving love. Speak and act from the place of love within. Before making any choice check that it is in line with your new empowering belief. Choose love rather than fear every time.

9 Affirm your new belief through written statements and through speaking it aloud. Construct statements using the present tense, such as 'I am opening to happiness' or 'I now attract money for my highest good'. Spend 21 days writing down your chosen statement 21 times each day.

Why not say 'yes' to those things that are in line with your new belief and 'no' to the things that are not? Begin to empower your beliefs with the words you speak. Choose to speak only from the place of power that is within you, otherwise practise silence.

10 Take action on your new thought as if it were already true. Small achievable acts towards your goal help to change your beliefs slowly, whereas larger leaps of faith can speed up the process. Usually it is wise to go at a pace that helps you to extend your familiarity zone gradually.

11 Look for evidence in the world that helps you believe in the possibility of your new thought being true. Look for new information in the outer world and begin to look in new and unusual places.

12 Find some support and try to be with people who support your new belief until it is able to take root. If your belief is related to being more joyful, seek out people who are joyful and hang out with them for a while.

13 Ask Your Higher Self for help – through prayer, meditation or mental requests – to change limiting beliefs. Your Higher Self knows you intimately and is able to help at a pace in line with your path of growth. In asking for help always come from your still centre rather than from any sense of desperation.

## Meditation to Change Beliefs

*Firstly, be sure about the area you wish to change and state it clearly to yourself before beginning – for example, 'I am willing to discover my limiting beliefs about money.'*

*Then sit comfortably, close your eyes and begin to be aware of your cycle of breath. Notice the in-breath and the out-breath and the pause in between. With each breath allow relaxation to flow into your body, emotions and mind; let go of any tension. Breathe in light and allow this light to wrap itself around you. Step through the light and find yourself standing at the top of a spiral* staircase that descends into the earth. Go down the staircase; when you reach the bottom you may find a corridor and at the end of the corridor you may find a door. If so, stand in front of the door and notice how you feel. Behind the door you may find a landscape or the interior of a building – whatever you find will symbolically represent your beliefs in your chosen area. When you are ready, step through the door, close it behind you and begin to explore what lies ahead. Allow images to come to you, rather like turning on a TV and allowing the images to appear. Just let go and trust your Basic Self to communicate with you. Explore the landscape and note all the symbols that seem meaningful to you. Now begin to interact with the landscape and change, repair, heal or destroy anything that you feel represents your old and limiting version of reality.

Be as creative as possible; you can build a bonfire and burn any rubbish you find, or perhaps repair a building by calling in some helpers. If you are in a garden you can call in gardeners to pull out any weeds, prune the shrubs or plant something new.

Invite new symbols into your landscape – some beautiful flowers, a sacred statue or a fountain. If you need more boundaries in life, build a wall or put locks on the front door and put the key in your pocket. Make all the changes you need to.

When you are ready to leave, retrace your steps through the landscape, leave through the door and climb up the staircase. Be aware of your breathing to bring you back to full waking consciousness.

Write down your journey, noting everything that happened.

This process can be repeated a number of times until your new beliefs start to take root.

# Entering the Void

Working with beliefs takes courage for it means facing all the hidden blocks that exist within the self. A lot of confusion, self-doubt, self-hatred and fear may be attached to these blocks and it takes courage to ride the emotions that arise when changing beliefs. When we let go of our old ways of viewing life, some people who liked our old views may leave because they may not find us much fun to be around any more. This can be a testing time when we learn to separate from the views, opinions and judgements of others and stand alone in our own new worldview. Now is a time when others may see us in a different light – some may perhaps perceive us as selfish, misguided or uncaring, while others may find us inspired and purposeful. When beliefs are changing, the old familiar contours of how life is begin to shimmer and dissolve and then reform. Some people and situations may start to drift away and new ones may be at the point of entering. This is the stage of the Void, and we may pass through it slowly or quickly. This time may not always feel pleasant, familiar or comfortable but it is the time of greatest possibility, when the rules of the game of life begin to shift in line with the work we have done. We will enter this realm many times and in due course will begin to welcome it for it heralds a time of transformation.

# 5 INNER TRANSFORMATION

> *It is a basic principle of spiritual life that we learn*
> *the deepest things in unknown territory.*
> *Often it is when we feel most confused inwardly*
> *and are in the midst of our greatest difficulties that*
> *something new will open.*

Jack Kornfield

## Healing and Transforming the Basic Self

### *Allowing the Emotions Full Expression*

Our emotions are the different frequencies of energy that move through our body and its encompassing energy fields. They are the fuel that propels us through life, what makes us fully human. All of our emotions arise from the great polarity of love and fear that governs this universe, so they will have either a contractile or expansive feel to them. Although all emotions exist in this continuum there are no good or bad emotions. Take fear for instance. If you were sitting on a railway track and a train was hurtling towards you, you would need something to prod you to get out of the way. At that moment fear would have a use. But a more common scenario is sitting worrying about things that might never happen, and in this instance fear has no useful purpose at all. Fear is also an energy that is very close to the feeling of excitement, and this is often why people become addicted to watching horror movies. Fear is one way that the Basic Self seeks to communicate its needs to us, and we ignore it at our peril. An important principle that I uphold is that expressing an emotion tends to have an enlivening effect and repressing an emotion tends to have a deadening effect. This seems to be the case whether the emotion is rooted in fear or love. Anger can be expressed without blame and can help clear away procrastination and set appropriate boundaries. Anger is a wonderful energy yet, like a forest fire, it can burn destructively so needs to be handled with respect. When I am angry about something I find it helpful if I do not react immediately to a situation but first acknowledge I am angry and then express my anger as clearly as possible and without apportioning blame. Taking responsibility and owning anger is a key step in appropriately communicating it. Anger can be expressed to clear the air, to put a stop to being dishonoured, or to hurt and punish other people. The motivation behind its expression will determine how it is received.

What is not so often considered is the damage done by not expressing love. This can happen because of a fear of intimacy and possible rejection, yet the price of not communicating love will be a heart that is closed. Every time we turn from expressing love, warmth and gratitude we miss an opportunity to open our hearts to others. Unexpressed love can turn toxic and lead to frustration and even feelings of bitterness. It is important to let people know that we love them for being just the way they are.

Many of us have been taught that there are 'good' or 'positive' emotions (such as happiness and joy) and 'bad' and 'negative' emotions (such as misery and sadness). How emotions are labelled will differ from family to family and culture to culture. For example, one family may classify excitement as 'positive' and another may see it as 'negative', and one culture may not encourage tears or grief whereas another will give them special importance. In dysfunctional families where the members are required to shut down their feelings and never talk about family issues, strong inhibitors are placed upon the expression of certain emotions. Some families may classify being emotional as weak and being intellectual as strong. A sense of shame may become attached to expressing certain emotions and this will lead to them being consciously suppressed. But such suppressed emotions never really go away; they always seek to be expressed and integrated in some way. Suppressing our emotions uses a lot of our mental, emotional and physical energy, causing us to feel physically tense and emotionally drained. It also tends to diminish our innate power. Illness is one possible result when there seems to be no other way out. On the other hand, expressing our emotions can greatly reduce feelings of anxiety or numbness, and just the act of seeking to be more aware of what is suppressed paves the way for the expression and release of this pent-up energy. All of us are likely to be suppressing a certain amount of our energy and yet we may have done it for so long that we have forgotten what it is we are shutting out of our lives. No matter how strong the emotional storms, tremendous healing will result if we allow this energy to flow through and out of us. Allowing rage to flow uninhibited through the body, without reacting to the feeling as it is passing, is like watching an electrical storm over the ocean. Have you ever noticed that after the most violent storm comes the most peaceful dawn?

Richard connected with his emotional self through clowning. He discovered clowning shortly after giving up his accounting career with Reuters. Richard had never taken part in drama at school or university and so being attracted to clowning took him by surprise. As a ten year old he remembers being taken by his older sister to see Marcel Marceau, the great French mime, and was entranced by the strange beauty of his white face. In time Richard trained in sacred clowning, and this helped him to connect with his innocence, wonder and sense of magic. This style of clowning is far removed from traditional 'custard pie in the face' circus clowning and, as Richard explains, 'I soon came to love the playfulness and absurdity of the clown who finds magic in the most simple of situations. In this way I was able to explore my feelings of lack of direction, uncertainty and vulnerability. Clowning has greatly expanded my self-expression and spontaneity as well as encouraging my natural humour and joy.'

## Welcoming the Emotions

1 Go into silent meditation and devote at least ten minutes each day to noticing how you feel in the moment. Give permission for all feelings to surface. Censor nothing and greet each feeling as it arises. Notice if you habitually push away certain emotions.

2 Go into silent meditation and devote at least ten minutes to an emotion that you find difficult in other people, such as anger, frustration, grief or hatred. Look inside yourself and find the place where that emotion exists. Greet it and begin to accept this emotion. Make space for it and give it permission to flow through you.

## *Wellbeing and the Physical Body*

Modern medical understanding generally sees the body as a complex machine that goes wrong from time to time and therefore occasionally needs fixing. The main focus of modern medicine is on illness and its causes rather than on the conditions that give rise to wellbeing. This mechanistic approach to healing has tended to reinforce the idea that the 'patient' need not contribute to the healing process other than to agree to take the pills or undergo the recommended operation.

In the time of Hippocrates, one of the founding fathers of medicine, a physician did not focus just on physical symptoms but looked also at other factors, such as the social and living conditions of a patient. Thousands of years ago in the East, other models of healing were developed which understood the body as an energy system that existed within the context of other energy systems such as the environment and society. In almost all ancient approaches to healing and wellbeing there was no separation between body, consciousness and soul. As we have seen, the Basic Self is our elemental consciousness that creates the body anew each day without the help of its older sibling, the Conscious Self. If there are no pre-birth agreements that will manifest in ill health and if the Basic Self has been nurtured in an environment where it received positive messages about health, then it will naturally maintain radiant health. The Basic Self is always communicating to us through the body, by feelings of pleasure, longing and pain. Illness is a language that the Basic Self uses to communicate with the Conscious Self when something is going wrong. This language of illness is not meant as a punishment; rather, it is a means of communication that can be learnt and used to understand what is happening to the Basic Self. It is beyond the scope of this book to explore all the intricacies of this language. There are some excellent publications available on this subject, such as *You Can Heal Your Life* by Louise Hay and *Your Body Speaks Your Mind* by Eddie and Debbie Shapiro. The natural state of the body is one of radiant wellness, and being in the body is not meant to be a painful experience. It is possible to begin to communicate and co-operate with the Basic Self in its role of maintaining radiant health.

On one occasion a filling fell out of one of my teeth and shortly afterwards the tooth shattered and I felt some considerable pain. I sat in meditation and explained to my Basic Self that I would go to the dentist as soon as possible but in the meantime I wanted it to remove the pain. The pain left that same day and I remained pain free despite needing a couple of appointments over ten days to remedy the problem.

## Begin to Love Your Body

In the privacy of your own home find a large mirror and stand naked in front of it.

Become aware of your body and notice the things you like about it. Spend five to ten minutes just sending appreciation to the parts you love.

Then move on and scan the parts of the body you find dislike. Spend five to ten minutes just being aware of the feelings you have about these parts of your physical body. Then spend five to ten minutes sending love and appreciation to them. Be aware of any feelings that come up but just keep sending love and appreciation to those parts of your body.

## The False Self

In the modern world children are not always appreciated or cared for. In Britain alone, according to figures published by the Children's Society, up to 100,000 children run away each year, of which around three-quarters run away for the first time. Beyond this startling statistic lies the reality that many children are raised within a family where love is a scarce commodity. For some children the family may feel a very unsafe place to be, a place where they are exposed to physical, emotional or mental abuse. Such children usually conclude that the abuse is happening to them because they are bad, and that somehow they deserve it. Children who feel emotionally or physically abandoned will conclude that they are unlovable. Other children are brought up in an environment where rules (either implicit or explicit) dominate, and the price of breaking one of these rules is feelings of guilt, shame, self-hatred or punishment. Children are so easily conditioned to be 'good' or 'nice' if their parents' love is overtly linked to their behaviour.  For some, any feelings of fear and vulnerability become something to be ashamed of and are therefore hidden. If their innate need to be listened to has never really been met, these children will find it harder to flourish and they may start to feel they are somehow bad or unworthy. Some may feel guilty for just being alive. Some may react by becoming violent, seeking to strike out against a society that appears hostile and cruel.

These scenarios are all responsible for the creation of self-defeating, self-hating and highly self-critical adults, some of whom may not be able to function within a modern society. In order to survive, many children start to operate on automatic, handing over responsibility for their lives to a part of the personality that is constructed in the fertile soil of fear, pain and hatred. This part could be called the False Self, and it seeks to build defences and armour to protect us from the psychic pain that felt so overwhelmingly intolerable in our past. Its main job is to learn how to cope by denying or avoiding anything that triggers that original pain.

However, having such a False Self comes with risks because it is like a tenacious vine that wraps itself around the emerging consciousness. In some cases the vine may be so strong and prolific that it almost strangles its host. The False Self could be defined as a self rooted in a set of beliefs that say life is about suffering. This sets in motion an ongoing and automatic set of responses that seeks to escape that suffering. This self arises to protect the Basic Self while the Conscious Self is forming, yet it will inevitably strangle and prevent the development of an effective Conscious Self assuming its role.

This False Self develops in strength in line with the degree of trauma experienced in our formative years, and the more threatening the vulnerability seems then the greater the need for a defensive and armoured personality. This negative aspect of our personality is rooted in a belief in separation and it is responsible for all our hidden agendas, separatist beliefs around class, gender, religion and race – all the things that cause us to feel better or less than other people.

In order for the Conscious Self to grow, thrive and be effective in the world, the False Self must be cut away and completely removed and burnt. The False Self will seek to survive within you and it will fight and struggle against its demise, yet ultimately its roots must be uncovered and thrown on to the bonfire of inner transformation.

## Recognising the False Self

*The signs that a False Self is running within your life include:*

◆ *Feelings of self-importance or self-pity, feeling a martyr or a victim in life.*

◆ *Being driven, being a perfectionist or a control freak.*

◆ *Being habitually critical, rigid or judgemental.*

◆ *Constantly needing to compare and blame.*

◆ *Denying all personal responsibility in life and hiding behind excuses and confusion.*

◆ *Refusing to own emotions and then projecting feelings on to others.*

◆ *Taking life ultra-seriously, constantly worrying and having a constant need for certainty.*

◆ *An obsession with convention, tradition and formality.*

◆ *Living in the past or being lost in fantasies about the future.*

◆ *Wanting to feel special rather than feeling unique.*

◆ *Mood swings, or feeling meaningless or empty.*

◆ *An almost fanatical sense of being independent or a deep-seated feeling of neediness.*

◆ *Needing approval or being concerned with external appearances and status.*

◆ *Co-dependent and clinging behaviour.*

There is an ongoing debate between the spiritual camp and the psychological camp about this limiting personality. For almost everyone on the spiritual path the seeking of liberation from the False Self is a top priority, yet so often the nature of the False Self is misunderstood for it is often thought to be a product of the conscious mind. The approach of some spiritual paths is to ignore the mind and seek to transcend it. This could be compared with trying to do without our arms because they are injured in some way. In seeking to disown the mind it is inevitable that some form of loss of access to inner resources and personal power will occur. The psychological approach usually looks to building a healthy ego that can withstand the pressures and fast pace of modern living. In many ways this would seem a more practical approach than the spiritual, yet here the False Self is simply sidestepped and the Conscious and Basic selves are strengthened. This can work to some degree but it may not in itself be enough to clear away all the entanglements of the False Self. I have found that a path which blends both a spiritual and a psychological approach works well – the Conscious and Basic selves are supported and encouraged to develop and mature and at the same time the Higher Self is called upon to help clear away and transform the unhelpful patterns of the False Self.

Understanding and transforming our False Self is one of the major challenges of our time. Those people who have been reincarnated into families with a predisposition to ego problems have thus chosen to face this challenge head-on. Such families are fertile soil for criticism, fear, judgement and suppression, and perhaps even verbal, emotional or physical abuse. The decision by the incarnating soul to face difficult challenges does not in any way condone abuse or mean that it is OK if guardians do not take proper care of the incoming soul; it just means that there are some strong issues to be faced within the family and the incoming soul has accepted those challenges. In such circumstances the development of a False Self is consciously chosen in order to learn important lessons about the makeup of the False Self and the process of passing through its nightmarish labyrinths. People who manage to transform their False selves become the torch bearers for others who wish to do the same. Without an awareness of the nature of the False Self this aspect of the personality has free range within the psyche and can cause the Warrior to engage in fruitless battles and can also infiltrate the vision of the Priestess with fearful and self-hating imagery. It is important to remember that this part of us exists in a place of extreme fear and separation, although in its own way it is trying to help and protect us against a hostile world. With time, patience, love, conscious effort and the help of spirit, the False Self can be dismantled and its energy redirected through the Conscious and Basic selves for more joyful and useful purposes.

## *Ask Yourself*

*What grievances do you hold about your past? Who do you still blame?*

*What are you trying to prove? What blocks your happiness?*

*Where do you still want to be right? What are you afraid of?*

*What excuses do you use in life to defend yourself?*

*Where do you feel the need to feel special?*

*Where do you feel self-importance or self-pity?*

*Where do you feel superior or inferior to other people?*

*What leads you to feeling victimised in life?*

*What negative fantasies do you hold about your future?*

*What do you do to sabotage your life?*

## *Meditation to Clear the Mind*

*Once again find a time when you can be alone and undisturbed. Find a comfortable position and begin to be aware of your cycle of breathing. On each in-breath imagine you are breathing light into your spine and continue to imagine this until your spinal column is filled with light and shimmering along its whole length. Then imagine that your spine is so filled with light that it begins to spill over and ripple throughout your physical body. Allow the light to flow up into the head and down towards the feet until eventually your whole body is filled with light.*

*Imagine that your mind is a great crystal-like energy field that surrounds your body. Notice if your crystal is murky or clear.*

*Is it filled with any sort of debris? Notice if the crystal feels calm or disturbed. (Any murkiness may represent limiting or disturbing thoughts or energy blocks.) Imagine that you can call light to flow through your crystalline energy field and see a great waterfall of light pouring down from above and flowing through and around you. Allow the waterfall of light to disperse any murkiness until the crystal feels clear and sparkling. Begin to absorb some of the light so that your crystalline energy field seems radiantly bright and you feel clearer and refreshed.*

*When you are ready allow the image of the waterfall and crystal to fade away. Return to your cycle of breath and come back to full waking consciousness.*

## Transforming the False Self

*Begin to connect with your cycle of breath and imagine breathing in the light of relaxation and peace. Allow each part of your body to relax as you surrender to this peace and relaxation. Imagine yourself sinking into your inner world and open all your inner senses. Imagine in front of you a tall mirror in which you can see yourself clearly. Notice how you see yourself. When you are ready imagine that you can step through the mirror. As you do so it feels like stepping through a still and cool pool of water that ripples as you move through it.*

*On the other side is a landscape of great beauty. Mentally call out to your Inner Priestess to come and join you. Greet her and ask her to take you to the place of greatest fear within you. Journey now together through your inner landscape and notice how it changes as you go to meet the place of greatest fear within you. Step into this place, which may feel or appear very dark indeed. Explore this place and find a spot where it would be good to meet your False Self. Mentally call to this part of your consciousness and allow it to enter the landscape and move towards you.*

*When eventually your False Self stands before you, mentally greet it and spend a moment noticing how you feel about this aspect of you. Then ask your False Self what it has to say to you, and simply listen to its response. It may reply through anger, criticism, judgement and fear, but simply listen without reacting and stay centred and neutral. When your False Self has finished, thank it for what it is trying to do for you but explain that you are no longer prepared to live in fear and now want to live your life from a place of love and power. Allow your False Self to reply; remember, you do not need its approval to make the changes you wish in your life. Stay loving and heart-centred and feel the support and love of your Inner Priestess nearby.*

*The next step is to call in your Higher Self to work with you to change the vibration of the False Self. When your Higher Self joins you it begins to send light into the False Self so as to change its structure. Watch as light is pulsed into this part and wait for your False Self to transform its appearance into something radiant or positive looking. Eventually it transforms into a symbol. Take this image and absorb its energy into your body. Feel the energy ripple through your body, thank your Higher Self and, accompanied by your Inner Priestess, retrace your steps. At the portal between the worlds thank her for her help and pass through the mirror again and return to your body.*

> *Spend some time assessing your journey. When you meet your*
> *False Self for the first time it may be a little shocking to realise*
> *that you hold such a level of attack and limitation within you. It is*
> *important to know how your False Self attacks you with its*
> *messages. This journey may need to be repeated a number of times*
> *to ensure a lasting impact. The False Self may seem highly*
> *resistant to love at first but, with persistence, it will transform.*

## Open to Being Loving

> *We are shaped and fashioned*
> *by what we love.*
>
> Goethe

The quality of unconditional love from the Higher Self puts the False Self to sleep and works to undo the patterns that hold it together. This quality of love rarely exists in the outer world but is found in abundance in the spirit worlds. Love is the magic wand that transforms fear and separation. All of the great teachers have taught the value of love and compassion yet somehow we have got the message twisted and started to believe that loving another is more important than self-love. I have not found it possible to truly love another person if I hate myself. I have found that self-love (an unconditional positive regard for who I am) lays the foundation for loving others and opens the door to the love that my Higher Self has for me. Love is a quality that seeks to flow, yet it can flow through me only if my terminal is clear of resistance. Receiving love is a part of the circuitry of giving love, and an inability to receive will negate its flow. One of the sad symptoms of being caught up in the False Self is that we become programmed to close down and not to trust. Because of a fear of being judged or criticised, we may erect such strong defences that we shut off all possibility of intimacy. Love dissolves the hardness and coldness of the False Self and opens our hearts. Being open-hearted means feeling everything more deeply, and so we may feel both the sadness and the joy of the world more intensely. Love opens the door to being fully alive in the present moment, and ultimately it is all that exists. Start to believe in the power of love and begin now to practise putting love into action. Self-love includes the need for appropriate boundaries and it rejects all self-hatred or self-attack.

## Eliminate the Need to Attack

*The most damaging thing we can do to ourselves is to criticise others constantly, since all judgement is a form of self-attack. Judgement leads to blame, which can generate hurt, guilt, self-reproach, self-condemnation and self-hatred. When blame is expressed as an attack on another it can cause considerable pain for that person, even if this does not seem to be the case. Be aware of all the hurt and pain that lies behind all your judgements. Avoid using the language of blame such as 'You did this to me' and instead start to use language that owns your own feelings such as 'I feel … about …' Do not criticise yourself when you notice you are being judgemental; instead, pause for a while, accept how you are feeling and send love to the place that is hurting inside.*

*Practise a gentle awareness of your thoughts and feelings throughout the day. Notice when you begin to blame yourself or other people. Be honest and tell yourself the truth and acknowledge to yourself when you slip into blame. Taking some time out and contemplating the qualities of love and acceptance are the best remedies for blame and self-attack.*

*Make continual choices for self-acceptance and self-love and call a halt to the war within yourself. Self-acceptance opens the way to a real acceptance of others. It also makes available more energy for living and is a foundation for greater self-esteem and self-value.*

*Check out self-love and extend some loving kindness to yourself. How about opening your heart and giving yourself a much deserved break today?*

## Practise Gratitude and Appreciation

*Notice when you get lost in complaining about life or yourself and instead try practising gratitude and appreciation. Learn to dwell on everything you feel grateful for in life and begin to make it a daily practice to appreciate your body, emotions and mind. No matter how difficult your life circumstances, start appreciating your outer world – the flowers in the park, a smile from a stranger, an intriguing film or a beautiful poem. Then take a big step and start expressing your gratitude to other people. At first this may seem a little awkward but with practice is a great way to shift both your energy and your relationships on to a new level.*

*Notice where you are from moment to moment on the continuum of gratitude to complaining. Practise giving yourself and other people a break from complaining. Remember, pure gratitude cannot help but change your experience of life.*

# Open to Being Authentic

The False Self is adaptive; it adopts roles and hides behind masks in order to defend itself and to gain something from other people. Living through masks and roles can become a compulsive way of living, where all choice about how to be in life or how to respond to circumstances is negated. The False Self can put on masks of happiness or wisdom, success, of being smart, sorted or nice, or even of spiritual ecstasy if it sees a point in doing so. However, pretending to be something we are not inevitably leads to a state of inner confusion. Our False Self invariably seeks for us to be false in life since it knows no other way of being. The only way out of this unhappy predicament is to recognise the tactics of our False Self and then consciously begin to practise being authentic. This means constantly monitoring our habit of putting on masks. When we are aware of putting them on, we can then take them off gently and become true to ourselves. Being authentic cuts through the False Self like a laser through butter, yet this may seem a challenging thing to do if the False Self has been running the show for many years. For some people a False Self is so firmly rooted in their way of being that they have completely identified with it and may be frightened to trust that there is any other way. They may not be able to remember any experience of being authentically themselves. In a way this is like an actor who is so absorbed in his performance that he has lost all sense of his true identity. Taking off the masks of the False Self can be frightening since it may mean facing our fear that nothing really exists behind the False Self. Authenticity means becoming more 'real' in our dealings with other people and behaving in a way that is congruent with our values and standards. It takes courage to move beyond the limiting behaviour and attitudes of the False Self into the truth of our being. This reminds me of a joke I once read in a book by Robert Holden. Two caterpillars see a butterfly pass overhead. One caterpillar turns to the other and says 'You'll never get me up in one of those things'!

## The Masks of the False Self

*Do you ever wear the mask of being nice to gain other people's approval?*

*Do you feel the need to 'look good'?*

*Do you ever wear the mask of helplessness or hopelessness?*

*Do you ever feel the need to wear the mask of the perfectionist or the control freak?*

*Do you hide your true feelings?*

*Are you able to be vulnerable and intimate with people?*

*Can you be yourself?*

## Breaking Old Masks

This exercise is similar to the one given in Chapter 1. Again, you will need a piece of card or paper big enough to cover your face. A paper plate will do if there is nothing else to hand. With this you can make a mask that represents any role you feel stuck in. Gather some art materials – crayons, paint, feathers, beads, coloured wool, glue, glitter – whatever you wish. Spend some time in silence meditating on this role and notice how you feel about it. How disempowering is it, and how much does it rob you of choice? Set aside some time to make this mask when you will not be disturbed. As you make your mask allow all of your emotions about this role to pour out into it. If any words come to mind then simply speak them into the mask. Take your time and when you are finished sit with your mask and notice how you feel about it. Are you ready to release this old way of being? The mask can later be burnt in a sacred ceremony to celebrate the release of this role. This exercise can be done alone or with a group of friends who wish to go through the process together.

On another occasion repeat the exercise, but this time make a mask that represents a positive quality to replace the role you have released. This mask can be placed somewhere in your home or garden to remind you of your radiant inner power.

## Working With the Shadow

> People say that what we are all seeking is the meaning for life.
>
> I don't think that's what we're really seeking.
>
> I think what we're seeking is an experience of being alive.
>
> Joseph Campbell

In the False Self's ongoing attempt to fashion its host into something that will be accepted and approved of, it seeks to banish any parts that it thinks either the family or society finds unacceptable. These discarded parts go into something that Carl Jung called the Shadow. In magical circles this aspect has been called 'The Dweller on the Threshold' because it exists within the deepest regions of the unconscious, the most inaccessible place of the Basic Self. This part of us is there to catch all the bits and pieces that we attempt to disown or jettison from our consciousness. This part starts to develop when we are very young and is there to catch both 'negative' and 'positive' attributes, talents or emotions. This happens because somehow as we grow up we come to believe that certain parts are dangerous, disgusting, shameful or useless – and so we send a message to the Basic Self to take away these bits of us. And this is what the Basic Self does, although because it can never get rid of a part of itself, it just hides it away somewhere in the deepest recesses of its being. Once thrown away into the Shadow this bit of us is no longer available to our consciousness, although the Shadow waits to return it to us when we are ready.

I heard a story a few years ago, in an open-sharing session of a personal development seminar, that I remember to this day. The man who told the tale had two daughters, both of whom were artistic. One day when he came home one of his young daughters proudly showed him a wall in the house that she had painted with all sorts of bright colours and images. The man was upset and told her never to do that again. He shared his regret for having said that because that daughter soon after lost interest in any artistic pursuits whilst his other daughter went on to use her artistic abilities in a professional capacity. This case illustrates how a positive talent can be discarded into the Shadow.

In practice what this means is that when we were young we may have received the message, either directly or implied, that certain things –

such as being too clever, too bad, or too angry, too excitable, too sexual – were not acceptable. This may have occured because our parents had not been very successful or happy and so such qualities had to be disowned. To have expressed certain talents or emotions would then have felt like a form of betrayal. Today, when artistic ability tends to be devalued, it is easy for parents to encourage their children to disown such an ability so that they do not become sidetracked from pursuing a 'proper' career. Similarly, it is possible to discard weakness into the Shadow and then the mask of the False Self will be one of a super-independent and capable person who never shows any sign of being weak or wrong or needy. When greed is discarded the individual concerned may express herself as ultra-caring and never allow herself to think about her own needs. If inner power has been discarded then the main mask can be one of playing a victim in life. Throwing away any trait into the Shadow leaves a sense of emptiness and imbalance, and our modern way of living seems to encourage the development of the Shadow. A shamanic teacher of mine once said that many families 'demand soul loss from their children'. This is not because they want their children to suffer, but families that have collectively suffered soul loss are dysfunctional in one way or another and children of such families get the message that they must conform and adopt this way of living also. Naturally we all come in as unique beings and so this process is not identical for everyone, yet without awareness of the Shadow bits of us will inevitably get lost. These Shadow parts need to be returned if there is ever to be any sense of wholeness and growth. We must embrace our lost anger, jealousy or arrogance, for example, in order to feel the totality of who we are. We need to reclaim any lost talents that we discarded because of a fear of being too smart or too anything. Like the Basic Self, our Shadow is our ally and wants to be helpful and return to us our hidden storehouse of treasures in order that we may feel whole again. This modern-day psychological concept has long been known to those living within indigenous, tribal, shamanic-based cultures. The ancient wisdom of these cultures held emotional, mental and physical illness to be a result of soul loss, which was seen as a condition where some of our vital essence has fragmented and split off, usually because of some kind of trauma. It has also long been known that soul loss leaves in its wake a sense of emptiness, alienation and separation from the web of life. Soul loss can happen at any time but we are especially susceptible if, during childhood and adolescence or as a young adult, we experience feeling abandoned, some form of loss, pain or shock, or any kind of abuse. Shamans would also say that parts of our soul or vital essence can be frightened or stolen away, leaving us with a sense of being incomplete and not fully alive. Classic signs that soul parts have fragmented and split off include: an inability to remember whole segments of the past, a feeling of not being whole, numbness, illness, feeling isolated and alienated, an addictive personality, a sense of inner emptiness, a feeling that there has been a fall from grace, low self-esteem, chronic depression. Soul loss and the development of the Shadow are one and the same thing, although psychology and shamanism disagree on some of the finer points, such as where the 'lost' part of our consciousness has gone: in psychology it is thought to be discarded within the unconscious and in shamanism it is thought to be hidden in the spirit worlds.

I have worked within both systems of calling back the Shadow and working with soul retrieval. Both work well and can bring dramatic results.

An important feature of the Shadow is that it will try to grab our attention in order that the process of returning the parts can begin. The Shadow does this by attracting people to us who display the talent, emotion or characteristic that has been lost. So if aggression and hostility have been disowned we will attract lots of angry and violent people into our life; if magic has been disowned we will attract lots of people interested in metaphysics or the occult; if fear has been disowned we will be surrounded by lots of fearful people, and if success has been disowned we will have successful people right in our faces. If the people we attract are displaying a 'negative' trait we may wish them to leave, yet such people may hold a certain fascination for us as well as provoking feelings of disgust, envy or repulsion. These are the same feelings that seek to keep this inner Shadow part at bay. If they are displaying a 'positive' trait they may evoke feelings of admiration and wonder and the conviction that they are more amazing than we could ever dream possible. The point is that all of these people are merely mirrors of the Shadow within and are therefore helpful pointers towards the path of wholeness.

## Meeting and Integrating Lost Shadow Parts

*Sit in meditation and connect with your still centre through the breath.*

*Open all your inner senses and imagine yourself standing in a beautiful landscape. Call to your Higher Self to be with you. Wait until you feel it has arrived and then ask this part of you for help in working with your Shadow.*

*Your Higher Self will then turn and lead you on a journey. Follow it as it takes you deeper into the landscape until eventually you arrive at a building – anything from a ruined abbey or a fortress to a beautiful cottage. It may even appear as a house you once knew or lived in as a child. If your Higher Self takes you to another place then that is fine. Always follow what your Higher Self presents to you. If you come to a building follow your Higher Self into it and begin to explore together. Look for any lost parts that are there. They may appear as small children, animals or very strange-looking beings. Check all of the floors, especially the basement, and on each one check with your Higher Self to make sure that the part you find is one you need to bring back – you*

*may just get a feeling of 'yes' or 'no'. When you have finished and*
*have gathered everyone up, follow your Higher Self to a healing*
*place, either inside or outside the building. Here your Higher Self*
*will begin to surround all of the parts you have collected with*
*light. Just watch this happening as more and more light is woven*
*around them. Then move into the light and allow these Shadow*
*parts to step inside you one at a time and merge their energies*
*with yours. (Some may be taken away by the Higher Self for*
*healing and so will not step into your energy field. These can be*
*integrated at a later time.) When all are merged thank your*
*Higher Self and go back the way you came through the landscape.*
*Return to your breath and then to waking consciousness.*

After consciously calling the Shadow to restore lost bits of consciousness, then meeting it and taking back those parts, comes the essential period of integration. This can take months, and for this reason it is important to take this work at a pace that feels comfortable. Having too much returned at once can feel overwhelming and this is why the process is overseen by the Higher Self. The returning soul parts bring back with them all the memories and psychic pain that caused them to leave in the first place, and this needs to be consciously embraced. (Imagine that a long-lost relative suddenly shows up on your doorstep and wants to tell you his life history, perhaps digging out loads of supporting photographs. If you showed little interest he may decide to pack up and leave once more.) It takes a little time to get acquainted with a returning soul part – and for the part to feel reassured that it is safe. Once integrated within the Basic Self all its energy and latent abilities become available once more.

The strongest soul retrieval I ever experienced happened spontaneously during a very intense week-long personal development course that took place in a residential centre in Devon. One morning near the end of the course I woke up feeling very strange and I found it difficult to say very much. I went into meditation and opened my inner vision and saw that a soul part which looked to be between three and four years old was approaching me, wanting to return. This part looked very innocent, wide-eyed and beautiful; he was dressed in an elfish silver garment and was holding an enormous flower. I spent around three months welcoming and integrating this part; it brought back many memories and feelings that I had lost touch with. The return of this part led me to feel more connected and alive. Working with the Shadow is perhaps the most powerful and most needed healing required in our modern-day way of living.

## *An Invocation to the Higher Self*

*I call to you my beloved self, the dweller at the core of my being – come and be with me as I journey through my life. Be with me throughout this day as I engage in the world and be there at my side as I step into the dream state. You are the Shining One that sets my path alight with inspiration; you show the way through the entanglements of my False self; you untangle the knots of my mind that block out love.*

*You are the Shining One that burns within my heart; you set me on fire with your love. Come and enter the pool of my emotions and pour your light into the places where I hurt most.*

*You are the Shining One that lights my path; flood your light through me and wash away all hindrances. Show me the way to grow through joy and delight, and untie the cords that bind me to struggle and suffering. You are the Shining One that knows the unity of all existence; I ask that you restore my consciousness to its rightful place in the web of all things.*

# 6 THE WEB OF ALL THINGS

*Only when the last tree has died, and the last river*
*has been poisoned, and the last fish has been*
*caught will we realise that we cannot eat money.*
Cree saying

## The Web

We have taken a look at the nature of the psyche yet this is only one side of the equation. We are not isolated pods of consciousness that float like flowers in some great cosmic pool; rather, our essential nature is one where we are connected with all things. For millennia humans have sought to attune with their environments through ritual, ecstatic dance, hunting, shamanic journeying and prayer, and have expressed their respect and regard for nature through art, social organisation, mythology and spiritual practices. Our ancestors felt the spirit of the land and thanked it for its gifts. In order to feel fully alive, empowered and free it is important to understand the innate interconnectedness of all things and how spirit is woven into the fabric of everything that exists. Shamanism, the spiritual path of most indigenous tribal peoples, had a term for this state of interconnection – 'the web'. Spirit weaves the web through the inner worlds of consciousness and out into the world of form. Within shamanic communities there was always an appreciation and desire for balance and harmony and an awareness of what brought disturbance to the web. We exist in a state of harmony when we feel both connected to the unseen realms of spirit and grounded in a sense of community and purpose in the world. The web is created and sustained by spirit and we are but guests on its strands. Often we are the ones that cause the greatest disturbance to the web, when we forget that we are connected to it and when we are pulled by the consciousness of the False Self.

Our Basic Self (our earthy, elemental side) is nourished and nurtured through its connection with the kingdoms of nature and by all the different energy fields emanating from the planet. Our Conscious Self is nourished and nurtured through social interaction and an experience of beauty and purpose in the world. Our Higher Self is nourished by the process of growth and is the part of us that experiences a state of ongoing connectedness. Connection to the web is our natural state of being. As children we knew and felt this, yet in our modern world the risk of disconnection is great. We enter the world as spiritual beings, and one of the most painful lessons is learning how to pass through the experience of disconnection. At some point in the evolution of our consciousness we will all pass through the doors of this dark challenger. If there is a definition for evil it comes from this state of being lost and cut off from the unity of consciousness within the web. This mystical feeling of connectedness is the natural state of our being and once touched this blessed state is never forgotten.

## The Threads Within Nature

*The natural world is the larger sacred community*
*to which we belong. To be alienated from this community*
*is to become destitute in all that makes us human.*
Thomas Berry

We live in a time when there are many challenges facing humanity – climatic changes, conflict around the planet, the depletion and destruction of planetary resources, the extinction of plant and animal species, famine, population growth, pollution and poverty.

Many futurists, scientists and social thinkers seem to believe that we are facing an evolutionary crisis. Our planet seems to be sending us many messages about how we are living and using its resources. If we ignore these messages we will eventually hit a global crisis. For too long our planet has been seen as just something to use rather than as a sacred and holy place deserving of the utmost respect. This in part has come about because of a belief that spirit and matter are separate and therefore we can use the resources of the earth in any way we see fit. For many centuries different religions have preached a philosophy that matter is somehow tainted or even evil and that the body and its senses are something to be transcended and the land is something to be controlled. In its own way science has helped to develop a psychology of separation and superiority in which the earth is seen as nothing more than a container of resources that can be used and then thrown away. The earth is being stripped of its resources in order to feed an insatiable consumerist market where some have considerable access to these resources and others do not. This dishonouring of the earth needs to change since every action has consequences and as we damage the earth we cannot help but damage ourselves.

Many indigenous tribal peoples believe that our planet and all the kingdoms of nature are totally imbued with the loving radiance of spirit. Such a worldview allows them to experience the nurturing and healing spirit within all things. The earth has long been seen as sacred; the planet was likened to a great Mother who nurtured everyone that lived there, and harming Her was sacrilege. In Britain, the Celts and the ancient people before them had a great appreciation for the earth and honoured the sacred places of the Earth Mother. They felt and traced the dragon or ley lines, where the life force of the earth flowed. These lines were often marked with great stones and some places were so powerful that stone rings were built to mark them (as at Stonehenge in Wiltshire in southern Britain). Some of these places seem to radiate a masculine feel and others are more feminine. Every year I usually set some time aside to visit the sacred sites of Glastonbury in Somerset, which I feel is my spiritual home. The red Chalice Well and its beautiful healing gardens have for me a strong, earthy, feminine feel, whereas Glastonbury Tor, with its Druid labyrinth and ancient tower that juts up into the skyline, has a stronger, masculine feel. The ancient peoples of this land honoured and celebrated the mystery and power that they saw all around them and knew the magic that existed within animals, plants, rocks and trees. They could hear the silent whispers of spirit in their dreams.

Although we now live in a very different world, that same ancient power slumbers within the landscape. This power is benevolent – despite being much maligned by religion and almost totally ignored by science – for it is an aspect of the spirit of all things. We have forgotten the old ways, labelling them as primitive, and have sought to tame the wildness of the world in order to make it conform to our idealistic notions of a safe and cosy environment. Such a global attempt to control and subdue nature would have horrified our ancestors, who knew that the outer world was but a reflection of our collective inner world. Seeking to tame the wildness of nature and attempting to destroy the many species of wildlife we classify as dangerous or a nuisance will result in something changing or dying within us. In Britain many species such as bears, boars, wolves and cranes once freely roamed the landscape. These creatures no longer share their gifts and beauty with us in the outer world, although they still call to us from the spirit worlds.

For the city dweller whose experience of nature goes no further than visiting the local park, sitting in a garden or having a few plants around the house, the wildness and power of nature can never really be touched. Wild places are untamed and free and as such can be restorative, helping us to reconnect with the wildness that exists within our own being. The False Self grows very strongly within the 'civilised' world and this civilised veneer seeks to keep us nice, numb, controlled, driven, and acceptable to society and its values. It may not like very much the part of us that seeks to be fully alive and unfettered and free. The False Self cannot understand or feel the deeper rhythms of life, nor can it comprehend the thrill of lightning as it strikes the earth, the consciousness that directs a flock of birds in flight, or the whispers of the ancestors that call to us from the rocks and waters of the earth. Our wild self knows a different kind of power, one that is linked not to salary or status but to the throb and flow of life and the wonders of the earth. This self knows the pure innocence of play and the ecstasy of the sexual energy that flows through the body. This feeling of ecstasy connects us with our body, our most intimate link with the physical world. Living in the modern world has many benefits and joys yet it can also leave us feeling bombarded with information, opinions, statistics and imagery. This can leave us in a kind of hypnotic haze where we can take on board limiting beliefs about nature, seeing it as threatening, primitive or dangerous. We may even see the earth as some vast prison for wayward souls, or perhaps inherently evil or hostile. Today's world can keep us busy and distracted and encourage addictive and co-dependent behaviours that keep our inner wildness well at bay. Living in such a way we are at risk of losing our ability to live fully empowered in the present moment. Now is the time to remember the ways of our ancestors and consider the impact of our actions on the generations to come. It is time to heal and honour the sacred earth once more.

I asked William Bloom, best-selling author and metaphysical teacher, what he thought about this subject, and this is what he said:

> *I was born and brought up in the centre of London. As a child and teenager I found the countryside and even the seaside boring. Where was the action? Where was the entertainment and the buzz? I liked rock and roll, nightclubs, motorbikes and having fun.*
>
> *Then I met a woman who was involved in the first Glastonbury Festival and through a strange series of mistakes she got the*

*impression that I was loaded and could help the festival financially. So she brought me down to Glastonbury. My only real interest was where my friends and I could park our motorbikes. Within 20 miles of Glastonbury, however, I began to feel a warm excitement growing in my body. I was being touched by some new vibration, which I really enjoyed. I could hardly believe it. I was taken up to the top of Glastonbury Tor and for the first time in my life I could sense and even see the great waves of sparkling energy that roll across and through the earth. Suddenly I was in love with landscape. Here was something to enjoy and explore and learn from for the rest of my life.*

*This change was so great that I finally lived for two years up in the High Atlas Mountains, with no plumbing or electricity, learning to enjoy the extraordinary companionship of nature. This is a relationship that I am still developing and deepening. The more I give attention to nature and the earth, the more I seem to receive and the more I feel strengthened and supported.*

# The Threads Within the Human Kingdom

*We will be known forever by the tracks we leave behind.*

Lakota Sioux saying

## Family Relationships

There is perhaps no greater poverty than feeling isolated and alienated in the world. Life can feel traumatic and painful at times and many people experience an ongoing state of disconnection from the love and support of their families and the wider community. Feeling disconnected can lead to a sense of closing down to life or a need to strike out at those who appear threatening and unfriendly. This feeling that the world is somehow hostile can start as early as in the womb, where we are highly in tune with how our mother feels about life. This is our first and most important relationship and it is important to have had a healthy and supportive bond with our mother since she is usually the person who introduces us to the web of human relationships. If no such bond occurs in the womb and in the early years, serious emotional problems can emerge later in life. The birthing process generally does little to reassure incarnating souls that they are entering a friendly and supportive world. Modern society, so long dominated by patriarchal thinking, has taken over the birthing process, once the domain of wise women and priestesses. There is also so much busyness and financial pressure on families that incoming souls may not feel sufficiently supported, nurtured or valued in their formative years.

It is within the family unit that we are nurtured and introduced to the web of human relationships, but sometimes things go wrong and the family is not a safe place to be. The parents may not be able to fulfil their obligation as guardians, and the children may learn to adopt coping strategies in order to attach to the web of human interaction. Communities within large towns and cities no longer enjoy the sense of cohesiveness that was once common, and some families feel quite isolated within society. It is important to have a sense of positive connection to the web of human relationships, and community is one of its vital threads. A community is no longer just our physical neighbours or the families we are born into; with modern methods of communication and transport it can include a widely dispersed body of people who are connected through bonds of love and mutual support. It is essential to build a community of people that encourage and support our path of growth, and with this in mind many people are now seeking new supportive networks.

## Sexual Relationships

Because they represent such a wonderful avenue for connection, sexual relationships can be seen as an advance class in growth. The honeymoon phase of being in love is a delight – as I'm sure those who have experienced it would agree – because it evokes a state of heartfelt connection with the beloved. Life becomes wondrous and magical and fear is for a time banished. Sexual relationships offer so much, yet without love and commitment sexual energy can also be used in an addictive and superficial way, which can exacerbate any sense of internal disconnection between the head and the heart.

Ashley, a good friend of mine, had this to say when I asked him about sexual energy.

> *In my struggle to evolve as a fully embodied and free man, time and time again I come back to my sexual energy and its place within the makeup of my soul. I know that this integral part of me is somehow a key to my finding true inner harmony. Many joyful gems and dark secrets lie hidden within my sexuality and digging deep into the rich soil of this part of my life has given me so much. Sex is a rich and beautiful part of who I am and I experience my sexual journey as a way of connecting with my body, psyche and, ultimately, with God.*

I agree with Ashley and I have learnt to tread the line between engaging with and misusing my sexual energy. Stereotypes of what it means to be a man or a woman seem to create unhelpful distortions that block true intimacy, since true sexual intimacy can occur only when we are in the moment, free of any expectations of how men and women *should* relate. Making love in a sacred way that honours the life force can open our vision to feeling the Divine in another and in ourselves. Sexual union builds energetic threads within the two energy fields of the lovers, thus binding them together in an energetic relationship. In a committed sexual relationship the auras of the two partners will in time blend and strengthen their connection, awakening their ability to communicate telepathically and heightening the rapport between them. However, inappropriate threads between ex-lovers can prove to be problematic unless consciously cut.

## Meditation to Clear Old Threads

*Sit in silent meditation and connect once more with the cycle of breath.*

*Come to your still centre and from there ask your Basic Self to help you sense all the threads that connect you to other people through a sense of guilt. Open your inner vision and begin to see and feel many tiny threads emanating from your body. These are the energetic threads that connect you to other people in a limiting way. Ask your Higher Self to begin to pulse blue/white light into your aura and then breathe this light in so that you become filled and surrounded with it. As you become full of light allow some of this pure energy to spill over and be absorbed into these threads. As more light flows through them they will begin to glow with this light. Now ask your Higher Self to begin to dissolve all these threads. Wait and watch as this light intensifies and begins to melt away the threads until they are all dissolved.*

*Then, either now or in a future meditation, ask your Basic Self to show you all the threads that connect you to other people through the energies of hatred, rage, shame, fear and pain. These can be cleared in the same fashion. When you are ready, return to the cycle of your breath and waking consciousness.*

*Repeat this meditation every day for one week so that your Basic Self gets the message to let go of all limiting threads.*

## Money and Work

These two commodities are wonderful vehicles for relationships within a community; however, they can also lead to feelings of failure, alienation, burnout and frustration.

Economic systems have tended to divide and define people on the basis of their usefulness or access to wealth. In the West we are now very poverty conscious, which I understand to be a state of mind where no matter how much money or how many things we possess we never have enough. So often it is thought that happiness will come with the next purchase or pay rise. In societies suffering from poverty consciousness, money can facilitate a greedy and ferocious consumerism that has no respect or regard for the earth and does not consider the impact of such a way of life on future generations. Prosperity consciousness is a state of mind, where wealth is seen in terms of stewardship rather than ownership, where there is a concept of having enough and sharing with others. Prosperity consciousness tends to place a high value on growth and spirituality; it sees everything physical – the body, money, property, even children and the life force – as being on loan. Poverty consciousness is a state of clinging where wealth is used to further self-interest and self-gratification. A gift given from poverty consciousness usually comes with strings attached. Prosperity consciousness gives freely without consideration of repayment, because a truly prosperous person knows that he or she is connected to an abundant universe where there is an abundance of life-force energy from which to create. True prosperity arises from a feeling of connection to the web. The web is all embracing and generous and gives freely from its vast storehouse of treasures (as is often said, 'the best things in life are free'). The prosperous person knows that whatever is given freely from the heart will return along the multiple threads of the web many times over.

Money is a strand of the web and is meant to be a tool to facilitate trade and exchange. In itself it is neutral and can be put to positive effect and produce amazing things. But it can also be used as a means to manipulate and control. For many on a spiritual path money can present many challenges – spirit and money have usually been seen as poor bedfellows. This split is illusory because money is a divine energy.

Work can be a wonderful way of connecting our passions with our talents; it also provides a fantastic opportunity to relate within a community. Work that fails to arouse our interest or passion and offers no possibility to engage and utilise our latent abilities is unlikely to be a deeply nourishing experience. This, however, is the unfortunate position of many within our highly specialised society. Such a situation inevitably leads to boredom, feelings of meaninglessness, depression, stress and isolation within the Conscious Self, and a sense of oppression within the Basic Self. Work can be the most empowering or most disabling influence on the Basic Self, for on a regular basis it involves a set of actions that reinforces a number of beliefs concerning self-worth, freedom, joy, creativity and self-love.

If work seems to lack what is important to us, then it is essential we ask ourselves why we are doing it. Are you telling yourself that you will change when you have an idea of what you want to do, and if so when will you know? Are you making a compromise between your need for security and your desire for fun and vitality? Work can be a way to uncover hidden talents and abilities, so that they can be played with in the world. Successful people are not usually bored or depressed by what they do; if they are then they will soon seek new pastures.

In the sphere of work often the focus is on the form of the work – such as being a teacher, doctor, soldier, sailor – yet it is the essence that we need to discover in order to then create the form. The essence is a latent talent or soul quality such as communication, healing or prosperity. Our Higher Self is interested not in what form our work takes but in the essence that we seek to awaken and express in the world. The essence, combined with ability, produces a line of action to take. What this means in practice is that when I combine what I have a passion for (ideas and spirituality) with what I know I'm good at (networking and business) I can then begin to look for the form. In my case I ended up being a director at Alternatives, where I put all of these to good use. The essence of our life work is known by our Higher Self and can be found through inner reflection and listening to the whispers of the heart.

## Your Life's Work

*This essence of your life's work is unique to you. This essence may involve communication, freedom, healing, love, personal power, peace, working with nature, or balancing your masculine and feminine energies. Perhaps your essence relates to being closer to spirit or helping in the awakening of other people.*

*It may be that the form of your life work has not yet been created on the planet, and so your task is to create it. If you are unhappy in your work make a commitment to yourself that you will take steps to change it. Ask your Higher Self for help in discovering the path of your heart and ask for courage and inspiration to step on this path.*

*Look at all the things you really enjoy doing and all the things you fantasise about doing. What qualities are you looking to awaken? Look out into the world and see all the people who you believe are happy in their work. Some of these people may be reflecting qualities you are waiting to awaken. Decide to discover your own unique gifts and talents and when you find any clues to these then nurture these precious seedlings within yourself. Do not allow discouragement to wither these latent talents and gifts. Believe in yourself and in the power that is within you to manifest your life's path.*

> *Thou askest me of what race, of what family I am;*
>
> *My mother is the beauteous Sun*
>
> *And my father — the bright Moon*
>
> *My brothers are the many Stars*
>
> *And my sisters — the white Dawns.*
>
> Traditional Slavonic song

## Our Racial Heritage

All indigenous tribal societies honoured their ancestral roots and gave thanks to those who had walked the earth and breathed life before them. The Basic Self is familiar with ancestral patterns through the DNA it receives from the physical parents, and any issue that was not faced up to or resolved satisfactorily by previous generations will be presented as something to be worked through. Many wonderful skills are also available through the bloodline since each racial group has successfully dealt with many challenges and awakened many abilities.

In our modern world there is a general failure to honour the ancestors and this has led to considerable problems. No longer do we remember our ancestors through songs or the recounting of stories around roaring fires. In some cases we may not feel very much gratitude for the legacies of pain and damage that have been handed down.

Within the collective consciousness there are many scars that remain to be healed; however, our racial inheritance can be worked with and where needed can be cleared very effectively with the help of spirit. This is a vast subject and I am able to touch upon it only briefly here.

# Connecting to the Web

> *The earth and myself are of one mind. The measure of the land*
> *and the measure of our bodies are the same.*
>
> Chief Joseph, Nez Perce

The quality of our connection to the web, both inwardly and outwardly, determines our state of harmony and wellbeing. When we feel troubled within the human community we can turn to the spirit of nature for help. Nature is free from negative ego issues and can thus give us much love and healing to help us transform and heal our sense of alienation, isolation and fear. Everything in the web of life is alive, has power and is responsive, and our consciousness is at core interwoven with all creation. This means we are never really alone. It is possible to live on a desert island completely isolated from the rest of humanity and still remain very connected to the web, as many mystics have discovered. Some people choose to remove themselves from the web of human interactions for a time so that they can more fully explore their innate connection to the web. For many today it is not possible or desirable to leave the world of human interactions for long periods of time, although short periods may be beneficial.

Since we are all connected we have a responsibility to the web in that whatever we send out through its threads will return. If we send love, joy and healing to others and hold a vision of the earth being whole, this is the energy that will come back to us. If we send out hatred, jealousy and resentment to others and hold visions that contribute to the destruction of our communities and planet, this is the quality of energy that will return to us through the web – eloquently expressed in the words 'As we sow so shall we reap.' Attacking another can disturb the web, as will allowing another being to invade or disrespect our personal space. Being a part of the web means that we can help to uplift the human family through thoughts and deeds of love, or add to its suffering by radiating, and reacting from, fear. Fear can give us the illusion that we are alone and unsupported, yet this is never the reality for consciousness cannot exist in total isolation from the Higher Self and the All That Is. The main work that we need to do is change the beliefs we hold in our consciousness about feeling separate.

We are all connected in the web at a consciousness and an energy level and this is why such things as telepathy and synchronicity are possible. This fundamental interconnectedness also means that spirit is able to reach into our world and communicate with us. This is something that has long been understood and appreciated by many indigenous tribal peoples who looked out for a communication from spirit through any unusual or significant signs and omens in the outer world. For those who know this mystery the outer world becomes like a giant three-dimensional tarot deck through which spirit can impart messages.

In my own life messages often present themselves in the outer world when I am at some sort of crossroads and need to make a decision. Once, when I was contemplating giving up my job, I began to look for some sign in the outer world. As I was walking down the road one morning and contemplating the decision I needed to make, my attention was drawn to a nearby house that had a sticker in the window saying 'Just Do It'. This message felt very significant and appropriate and as I continued on my way I found myself walking behind someone wearing a T-shirt with the same message printed on the back. Needless to say I resigned soon afterwards and I have never once regretted the decision. I only wish I had taken it earlier.

As we reconnect to the web of life all things are possible – we can find a path with heart, engage in work that we love, attract new loving supportive relationships, and find ourselves in the loving embrace of spirit. It is always possible to restore our mind, soul and body to their rightful places in the overall scheme of things, no matter how great the feeling of disconnection in the world.

## The Unity of the Web

*Sit and feel the spirit that resides at the core of your being.*

*Feel the light of spirit radiating from your heart chakra, the meeting place of the three selves.*

*Feel your connection to the web of life and thus feel the spirit that exists within other life forms such as an ant, a spider, a flower, a star or the sun.*

*Feel the pulse and rhythm of the earth and feel the light of spirit that flows through the sun.*

*Feel at the core of your being your divine spirit and see this divine light in everyone you meet. They are all sparks of divine energy within the great light of the God/Goddess force, and all the sparks come together in a unified field of consciousness. Feel the power of the web and let its power flow through you. Call on this power as often as you want for help and support.*

## Step into Flow

*Connect with the web and open to the flow of life. You will know when you are in the flow when things happen easily and effortlessly. Miracles can happen and may seem commonplace when you feel fully in the flow. The flow is experienced from the quiet inner centre, and from this place there is a coming into harmony with all other beings connected to the web. In the flow synchronicity happens and solutions appear in response to the challenges of life.*

*When we are in a state of disconnection it feels as if we are pushing the boat rather than flowing with the current of life. Struggle and suffering are sure signs of disconnection from the web. When struggle appears simply slow down and consciously come back to your centre and your place of inner stillness. Stay here for a while and consciously reconnect.*

## Connecting Through the Chakras

The chakras – energy centres that receive, assimilate and transmit life-force energy throughout our mental, emotional and physical systems – are our most intimate means of staying connected to the web. These centres form a rainbow bridge of consciousness that straddles our conscious, unconscious and super-conscious natures. 'Chakra' is a Sanskrit word meaning wheel or disk, and psychics report seeing these centres as spinning vortexes of energy. Symbolically the chakras have often been portrayed as flowers and in many ways they operate just like a flower, opening and closing according to the light and other environmental conditions. The chakras are housed within the etheric body, which is a non-physical field of energy that can be seen with the inner eye as a soft glow or haze around the body. The chakras distribute energy throughout the physical body and are centres of consciousness in their own right, being located roughly in line with the physical spine. They are connected by a vertical channel that runs from beneath the feet up to the top of the head and out beyond into the spiritual dimensions. These centres awaken in accordance with the growth we have achieved in other incarnations, our current age and the distance that has been walked on the path of growth in this lifetime. They can be roughly divided into lower and upper chakras, where the lower ones relate to the Basic Self and are more physically orientated and the upper ones relate to the Conscious Self and come under the sphere of influence of the spiritual dimensions. The meeting point for the upper and lower chakras is the heart, and it is this centre that is becoming more and more important in our present timeframe.

# Understanding the Chakras

## *The Lower Chakras*

**Base Chakra** – *In Sanskrit this centre is known as Muladhara, which means root and support. It is found at the base of the spine and its colour is deep red. This chakra regulates basic life-force energy and is associated with issues around physical survival. It is known as the Gateway of Earth. Crystals such as black obsidian and smoky quartz are good in healing and rebalancing this chakra.*

**Sacral Chakra** – *In Sanskrit it is known as Svadhisthana, which means sweetness. It is located in the lower abdomen and its colour is a tangerine orange. This chakra is associated with all the manifestations of desire, sexuality and pleasure. It is known as the Gateway of the Moon, since the moon rules it astrologically. Most orange crystals are helpful in healing and rebalancing this chakra.*

**Solar Plexus Chakra** – *In Sanskrit it is known as Manipura, which means lustrous jewel. It is found in the solar plexus and its colour is golden yellow. This chakra regulates metabolic energy and is connected to self-esteem, self-confidence and personal will. It is known as the Gateway of the Sun. Most yellow crystals, such as citrine and topaz, are helpful in healing and rebalancing this chakra.*

## The Meeting Place of Lower and Upper Chakras

**Heart Chakra** – *In Sanskrit it is known as Anahata, which means unstruck. It is located over the sternum and its colour is emerald green or pink. This chakra opens us to love, compassion, community and relationships. It is known as the Gateway of Wind, and crystals such as rose quartz, ruby, and most green gems such as emerald are useful in healing and rebalancing this chakra.*

## The Uper Chakras

**Throat Chakra** – *In Sanskrit it is known as Visshudha, which translates as purification. It is located in the throat and its colour is sky blue. This chakra regulates sound, expression, communication and vibration. It is known as the Gateway of Manifestation, and most blue stones, such as turquoise, are useful in healing and rebalancing this chakra.*

**Brow Chakra** – *In Sanskrit it is known as Ajna, meaning to perceive. It is located in the centre of the forehead and its colour is deep indigo blue. This chakra is associated with inner vision, prophecy, and envisioning the future. it is known as the Gateway of Light, and lapis and moonstone are useful crystals to help to open and balance this chakra.*

**Crown Chakra** – *In Sanskrit it is known as Sahasrara, which means thousandfold. It is located on the top of the head and its colour is amethyst/white. This chakra is associated with knowledge, understanding, higher thought and spirit. It is known as the Gateway of Consciousness, and amethyst, clear quartz and diamonds can help to open and balance this chakra.*

## Working with the Seven Chakras

*In meditation see each chakra as a flower bud on your spine that is ready and waiting to open. Imagine that you can breathe light up through your feet and into each bud. Start with the Base Chakra and see it open as a flower. The flower at the base points down and that at the crown faces to the heavens, all the others are horizontal. Breathe light up and open each chakra in turn until you reach the crown, and then just bathe in all the different colours that are flowing around you. This meditation can be reversed so that first you breathe light into the head and then you draw it down through each chakra to the base.*

*When you first start to do these exercises it is advisable to end each meditation by returning all the chakras to their original bud state. In time this may prove unnecessary.*

In working with the chakras it is important not to work too hard and force them to open too quickly. Just go with what feels comfortable and avoid exertion. In the West the Solar Plexus Chakra tends to be overstimulated because Western societies have long indulged in overdeveloping the will of the Warrior. This overstimulation of the will aspect tends to manifest as power struggles and conflict. For most people aligned to a Western lifestyle the challenge is to become more centred in the Heart Chakra and divert excess energy from the solar plexus to the heart. This is a challenge that many people are currently embarked upon. A more heart-based society would be less willing to make war on its neighbour and more inclined to stretch out a helping hand in times of need.

There is one further thing that is relevant to the chakras and how we connect to the web of life. It is one of the functions of the Basic Self to weave energetic threads from the chakras to connect us with other living beings. These threads are developed and strengthened through our relationships, whether with nature, other people or beings in the spirit worlds. These threads are helpful in anchoring us in life, yet they can also help to restrain us, especially when we seek to make changes. It is the nature of the Basic Self to hold on to the people and things it has forged energetic links with. Therefore at times it is necessary for the Conscious Self to step in and dissolve or sever these threads so that the whole self is liberated to move in a new direction. This process is well described in Phyllis Krystal's insightful and helpful book, *Cutting the Ties that Bind*.

There are two other chakras worth mentioning: the first is the Earth Chakra, which exists beneath our feet some way down in the earth itself. This chakra is our intimate connection with the earth and it is here that I have found the kundalini energy to reside. Kundalini is an energy that is usually said to lie dormant in the Base Chakra, yet I have never managed to find it there. This earthy energy lies coiled in the Earth Chakra and awaits the call of spirit before it begins its journey up the spine towards the Brow Chakra, at which point its host opens to what has been called enlightenment.

The other chakra I wish to mention is the Star Chakra, which is found between 18 inches and 2 feet (45–60 centimetres) above the head. This chakra opens to assist us in being more connected to the pulses of energy from the Higher Self, as well as acting as a sort of transformer of impulses of energy from other star systems. These two chakras are opening at this point in time because of the current growth of interest in spirituality and the desire to attain higher levels of consciousness.

An awareness of the chakras can be very helpful in opening sensitivity to the web of energy that permeates all living things.

# Grounding into the Earth

*Every step I take is a sacred step*

*Every step I take is a healing step*

*Healing, healing my body*

*Healing, healing the land.*

Pagan chant by Donald Engstrom

One way to connect with the web is to practise grounding into the energy systems and consciousness of the earth. Grounding can only be appreciated once the chakras within the etheric body have been opened and worked with. Grounding is a conscious sending downwards of energy in order to link with the vast energy body of the earth.

This is especially important for those people walking a spiritual path who find it difficult to engage with life and who have a tendency to 'space out'. Paradoxically, the deeper our connection into the earth the further we can fly into the realms of spirit. Grounding into the earth is also a great antidote for 'living in the head', one of the problems of living in Western society. It is essential to feel properly anchored into this physical plane and to be aware of any tendency to wish to escape from the responsibilities of an earthly life.

## Becoming Grounded

Find time to be in nature and sit on the ground or stand with bare feet. Use the cycle of your breath to come to your still centre. (If need be, this exercise can also be done indoors. It is a good idea to remove your shoes in order to allow a flow of energy through the soles of the feet.)

Begin to send your awareness down into your pelvic area and down into the legs and feet. Breathe in and then on the out-breath imagine you can send out energy roots from the soles of your feet down into the earth. Gather your energy on the in-breath and then on the out-breath again send your roots through the soil, mud and rock down into the earth. Continue to send your roots deep into the heart of the planet and find the place where the earth's rock turns to liquid fire. Push through this lava knowing that the heat will not harm you. Go deeper and find the tranquil heart of Mother Earth and feel the connection with the core of the planet.

Then begin to breathe up the energy of the planet through your roots. Draw it up on each in-breath as if you were drawing water from a well. Draw this energy up towards your feet and allow it to enter the soles of your feet. Breathe it up your legs and into your pelvic area, flooding it with the power of the earth. Then, when you are full, breathe it up into your belly and eventually bring it to your heart. Open your heart with this energy and then draw it up to the throat and eventually into your head. Allow this energy to flow out through the crown of your head and up into the heavens – eventually to cascade back towards the earth and be absorbed once again by the Great Mother.

Feel this flow for as long as you wish. Whatever energy you have within that you wish to let go of, simply surrender it to this flow. Welcome the heartbeat of the earth into your life.

When you are ready, simply come back to full waking consciousness, leaving your connection to the earth in place.

# 7 OUR UNSEEN FRIENDS

*If you want to ensure that you will never be poor and lonely,*

*seek silence, for true silence is inhabited by countless beings.*

Omraam Mikhael Aivanhov

## The Spirit Realms

Peoples from almost every land across the globe have in their time honoured and consulted with the spirit realms for guidance, help and healing. Shamanism, the oldest spiritual path known to humanity, has worked with the unseen friends in spirit for tens of thousands of years. Shamans have long been able to enter a state of altered consciousness and travel in the spirit worlds to meet with guides, healers and teachers, consulting them on a range of practical issues such as where they should look to hunt for food or how they should heal a particular illness. Although almost every religion seeks in its own way to connect with spirit, we are currently in a collective state of spiritual poverty and are in many ways further removed from the spirit world than our ancestors ever were. We live in a time in which science has created a wonderful array of technology and information, yet it could be argued that now more than ever we need the help of spirit to unravel the multitude of problems that has been generated by our modern age.

The spirit worlds are diverse and full of helpful beings that can share useful insights and wisdom about life and help us on our collective path of growth. Spirit exists within us, within nature and all living things, as well as in very separate dimensions.

## Working With Spirit

This book was written with the gracious help of unseen friends.

I would merely show up each morning at my laptop, place my writing crystal next to me and sometimes light a candle, and then I would simply wait for the unseen friends and my Higher Self to send me inspiration and ideas. Later in the day I would often receive information for forthcoming chapters or amendments that needed to be made to chapters already written. Sometimes I felt like a bystander watching the book unfold like a rose, never knowing how it would finish. This was not always an easy process for my personality self that worried about whether I could complete a readable book at all.

An important factor to consider when working with the spirit realms is the beliefs we hold about such contact. Beliefs that generate any fear or doubt can effectively block clear communication. It is important to check all beliefs held and to transform them so the Basic Self can open the door to such contact. Working with spirit is entirely natural; however, many of us grew up learning to fear the unseen realms. We believed they were places where no decent being would choose to hang out, because all the good souls were sent to that beautiful place somewhere above the clouds and all the wayward souls were pushed somewhere down below. In many cases religion itself has demonised the unseen and has effectively kept us afraid of touching spirit in ways not sanctified by the teachings of the priesthood. Science, which in its time has played a part in breaking up much religious superstition, has helped us to achieve more objective ways of looking at life and has brought much benefit. Yet science is so focused on measuring and quantifying the exterior world that the realms of spirit have been missed, for they do not easily fit under a microscope. Psychology has done much to explore the realms of consciousness but generally has developed its own jargon for dismissing spiritual ideas. However, both science and psychology in recent decades have begun to open up and embrace what was previously dismissed. Now there are branches of transpersonal psychology – as well as quantum mechanics theory – that are beginning to recognise the unseen.

In beginning to work with the spirit realms it is useful to clarify the reasons for doing so. Idle curiosity is a poor motive, whereas a passionate desire for healing, a desire to serve or a wish to find more meaning and purpose in life, is more sustaining. Strong motivation is needed in order to change from a seeker to a finder, and to enlist the co-operation of the Basic Self and move past any fear that it holds about such contact. Without this co-operation all communication is distorted to some degree or even blocked. Working with meditation is usually an essential step in opening the channel since meditation helps to create the inner stillness that enables the inner senses to open so we can see, hear, touch, smell and taste the spirit worlds. Imagination is the all-important doorway to stepping into these other worlds. It also enables us to receive and transmit telepathic communications from and to our guides and helpers. Imagination is often dismissed as simply the producer of fantasy, yet it is perhaps the most powerful tool available to us.

## The Two Modes of the Imagination

*Active mode – this is akin to fantasy where the imagination is employed in creative visualisation to construct and focus upon images or build an inner landscape in order to reprogramme the Basic Self with more helpful instructions. This mode is also used to send telepathic messages. It is like drawing or painting a picture.*

*Passive mode – this is used to open to sensing the spirit worlds and to receive messages or information from the Higher Self and the unseen friends. In telepathy, this is the mode for receiving. It is like turning on a TV set, tuning in to the desired channel and then waiting to see what images and sound come through.*

*With practice almost anyone can open and utilise these abilities and receive great benefit, and some people will probably find that they have a natural talent and passion for it.*

*No more words.*

*Hear only the voice within.*

Rumi

It is important to remember that we are totally safe in the spirit worlds and that we have our Higher Self watching over us always. Our Higher Self is the gatekeeper that watches over all the contacts we make with other beings.

Shamans know that everything in the physical world is alive, responsive and imbued with power. The consciousness of a crystal, a tree or the sun can be felt and known once sensitivity to them has been opened and developed. In the spirit worlds, beyond the physical, the guides and teachers can take many forms and may appear as a tree, an animal, another human being, an angel, or an other-worldly being. When working in the realms of spirit the rules of the outer world do not function in the same way. We may find trees that can talk, horses that can gallop over water, crystals that can bathe us in healing light, and eagles that can lift us and carry us great distances. Time does not exist in the same way that it does in the physical world, where it is so dependent on the rotation of the earth around the sun. And so time flows differently in the spirit worlds – things can appear instantly and crossing a landscape can happen in a few minutes, or even quicker. Often I lose all sense of time when journeying in the spirit world and later discover I have been away for much longer than I thought. For this reason it is a good idea to allow plenty of time to travel on inner journeys. Within the web there are many different expressions of consciousness and there is always an abundance of help available, no matter what the need. All we need do is ask for that help and open to the possibility that it exists. This help comes unconditionally, for the guides are usually only too willing to assist. I have found that meeting spirit guides or helpers leaves me with a greater sense of empowerment, wonder and connection.

Some guides may walk with us for a whole lifetime, guiding and watching over us; others may stay with us for a season or for a few years until their work with us is completed. In the spirit worlds we can also meet great master teachers who hold responsibility for the evolution of large groups of souls. Meeting such a being is a powerful stage in the process of inner growth and cannot be rushed. It is important to hold a strong intention to work only with the most evolved beings in the spirit realms for, as in life, not all the beings we may meet are fully awakened and wise. Anyone who has ever gone to a spiritualist church can tell you that being dead does not automatically make you a much wiser being. It is always important to be discerning when working with guides, even though they will never ask us to give up our power or follow their advice blindly. It is always worth checking out how any message feels intuitively before acting upon it. Useful questions to ask about any guidance from spirit is 'How loving is this information' and 'How uplifting does it feel?' Guidance may come in the form of reassurance or as information concerning action to take. The latter may feel a little frightening if it involves moving beyond our comfort or familiarity zone. But we should always remember that messages from the unseen friends are more like a stream of gentle and loving suggestions than a set of commands.

Working with beings that have passed through the veils of death helps to dissolve any fear about the death process itself and can help to transform any beliefs that the universe is fundamentally a hostile and unfriendly place. Through contact with the unseen friends we can begin to feel that we are never truly alone and that we have the support of many wonderful beings who are very happy to work with us.

The unseen friends include our own Higher Self, our most intimate guide and guardian angel. At a much higher level our greatest and most beloved guide is the Spirit of All Things. Our Higher Self and all other guides are but radiant sparks within the mind of this one.

## *Working With the Unseen Friends*

*You must have the desire for this work to happen and positive motivation, such as a desire to grow.*

*The way must be cleared, through changing any limiting beliefs and releasing any fear of contact in the Basic Self.*

*Then the space must be created for the work to happen, such as finding time to meditate and perhaps dedicating a space in your home for spiritual practice. Alternatively, spending time in nature can create the space.*

*It is useful to have persistence in order to build relationships in the inner worlds, in the same way that relationships take time and need nurturing in the outer world. Permission needs to be consciously granted to the unseen friends to open the way for them to assist you.*

*The contact can then be used for the uplifting of yourself and others.*

## Working With the Spiritual Community

There are many guardian spirits that can help to keep our vibration high and beings that work to help us root out and heal any pain we hold in our energy bodies. All the masters and wise ones who have ever walked the earth can still be met in the inner planes. Guides can help us with very practical life challenges and are also there to help us to navigate the inner worlds and find inner cleansing, healing, love, power and transformation. There are many beings that we can meet in the spirit worlds, such as nature spirits, power animal guides, angelic helpers, star guides and other-dimensional guides. At this time of great transition there are many beings that are keen to support humanity through the changes that lie ahead. In my belief system we are not alone in the cosmos and have been visited by star beings for many thousands of years. I encourage you to explore these realms and find out for yourself how useful contact with such beings can be. Do not be discouraged if this contact takes a little time to build, in the end the effort will be worth it.

## Meeting a Spirit Guide

*Begin to relax by connecting with the breath and allow the outer world to fade away as you turn inward and open your inner senses. Mentally count down from ten to one, and on the count of one imagine that you are standing in an inner landscape. Reach out and touch something and spend a few moments noticing this landscape.*

*Journey through the landscape until you come to a sanctuary or sacred place where you can meet your guide. Stand before the sanctuary and notice how it looks and feels before entering its grounds or gardens. Notice the beauty of this place and the vibration of peace and calm that exists here. Walk through the sanctuary until you find a large open space or hall.*

*When you are ready mentally call out to your guide in spirit to come and join you. Wait for this being to come, then notice the appearance and feel of this being. Your guide may appear as a human, a being of light or perhaps a being that is from the stars.*

*Stay with this being for a while and get a feel for his or her energy. When you are ready ask for a message and just wait and listen. Practise listening through your whole being – your mind, emotions and physical body. Perhaps this guide will communicate with you telepathically. Be open and ready to be surprised by what you receive. If you wish, telepathically ask your guide a question and wait for an answer. The answer may come through a visual or aural response or perhaps a feeling.*

*If there is anything you wish to know, ask now.*

*Ask for this being's name and his or her role in your life. Ask if there is anything your guide wishes to say to you. Is there anything your guide wishes to show you?*

*Stay here as long as you wish and when you are ready thank your guide and say farewell. Leave the sanctuary the way you came. Return to your breath and slowly come back to full waking consciousness.*

## Working With the Elementals

*I must shape my life out of myself –*
*out of what my own inner being tells me,*
*or what Nature brings to me.*
Carl Jung

Nature is completely conscious and alive and her many builders are the elementals – also known as fairies, nature spirits and the 'lesser builders', because everything that has form is built and maintained by these tiny beings. The elementals of earth, air, fire, water, spirit or life-force energy are to be found everywhere, working under the direction of spirit to sustain the physical world. So, for example, elementals of earth are to be found constructing the petals of a flower, working within the roots of a tree or helping to grow a crystal; elementals of water help to hold the shape of a drifting snowflake and they swirl in the power of a majestic waterfall; elementals of air move to form air currents and help to transmit the energies of sound; elementals of fire dart within a bolt of lightning, move within the circuitry of a computer terminal and flicker within the flame of a candle; elementals of spirit work to transport and transmit life prana or force energy to the etheric field of all living things. All these beings are also found within our physical bodies, working to construct and maintain all our systems under the direction of the Basic Self. Water elementals can be found working in the blood, lymph and digestive systems; earth elementals produce the organs, muscles, bones and tissue of the body; fire elementals produce the electricity within the brain and nervous system; air elementals work in the respiratory system; and spirit elementals work in the etheric field and chakras to help the flow of prana. Elementals are also present within our mental and emotional fields to construct and transmit thoughts and feelings.

All these beings are the children of nature that build our world of form and matter. They can be found everywhere across the planet – they are within the fabric of our cities and are especially strong in wild places such as deserts, forests, mountains and lakes where humans rarely visit. Gardeners with 'green fingers' who love nature will find that elementals flock to them to produce flourishing gardens. Elementals are powerful friends and are very helpful in matters concerning the purification, cleansing and healing of the body, mind and spirit. Although they are wonderful allies they are unlike other spirit guides in that they have a very different kind of consciousness, because they work within a group consciousness and under the guidance of what could be called 'architect' angels. Elementals work with humans, even when we are not conscious of their presence, and they respond to thought, will and love most of all. These beings can in many ways be likened to an electrical current that can be directed towards a positive, neutral or destructive purpose. Elementals are unable to offer the sort of help that many other kinds of guides can offer – such as guidance, wisdom or insight – but they can help with building a healthy body that is radiant with life-force energy, an emotional field that is tranquil, and a mind that is strong and clear and able to focus and concentrate. They are also an integral part of manifesting things such as a new project on the physical plane.

## The Elementals of Earth, Air, Fire, Water and Spirit

**Earth** – *corresponds to the direction of north and is the element of all things physical. It is the place of age, patience, prosperity, ritual, teaching* and wisdom. It relates to winter and death. This element is generally seen as being feminine in nature.

**Air** – corresponds to the direction of east and is the element of the mind. It is the place of the child and relates to spring, innocence, inspiration and birth. This element is generally seen as being masculine in nature.

**Fire** – corresponds to the direction of south and is the element of the will. It is the place of the adolescent and relates to summer, faith, relationships, strength and sexuality. This element is generally seen as being masculine in nature.

**Water** – corresponds to the direction of west and is the element of the emotions. It is the place of adulthood and relates to love, maturity, introspection, dreams and autumn. This element is generally seen as being feminine in nature.

**Spirit** – corresponds to the centre of the circle and is the element of ether, prana or the life-force energy. It is the place of transformation and rebirth, and it is both masculine and feminine in nature.

## Working With the Elements

Choose one of these elements and spend some time each day for a week meditating on either the symbol of the element or the statement associated with it.

**Earth** – Choose a symbol that represents this element to you, such as a mountain or a pine forest. Imagine that you can touch the trees or rock and smell the dampness of the earth. Alternatively, meditate on the statement 'I am silent.'

**Air** – Choose a symbol that represents this element to you, such as a blue sky, or the power of the wind. Feel the the air on your body. Alternatively, meditate on the statement 'I know.'

**Fire** – Choose a symbol that represents this element to you, such as the radiant sun or a raging bonfire, and feel the light and heat on *your body. Alternatively, meditate on the statement 'I will.'*

**Water** – *Choose a symbol that represents this element to you, such as a river or waterfall where you can touch the coldness of the current or feel the spray of water on your body. Alternatively, meditate on the statement 'I dare.'*

**Spirit** – *Choose a symbol that represents this element to you, such as a spiral or labyrinth, and feel yourself treading it. Alternatively, meditate on the statement 'I am centred.'*

*Every day for a week see the image before you and open to feel its power through all of your inner senses. If choosing to meditate on a statement simply open to feel the power behind the words and invite it into your life.*

## Inner Cleansing With Fire

*This meditation is useful if you feel you have internal baggage – physical, emotional or mental – that needs releasing. Fire elementals are very helpful in purifying the body, mind and emotions.*

*Sit or lie comfortably and find your way to relax and open to the inner worlds of consciousness. Connect with your cycle of breath and begin to open your inner senses and withdraw your awareness from the outer world.*

*Breathe in an orange light and allow this to fill your body, emotions and mind. Bathe in this orange glow. This light becomes a mist, which you can step through to find yourself in a fiery landscape. This place has in it an active volcano and you can see its glowing crater. The sun is high and radiant as you begin to journey towards it. Begin to climb up the volcano and feel its heat. When you reach the crater, look down at the landscape below and look down also into the fiery belly of the volcano. See the lava bubbling and casting a rich orange-red glow across the rocks.*

*As you stand at the top and look down, begin to get a feel for all the inner baggage you are carrying from your family. Imagine that you can ask your Basic Self to bring all this baggage to the rim of the crater. See a number of porters bringing up all this stuck energy, which could appear in the form of black bags or suitcases containing all your old junk. When you are ready, decide whether now is the time to release this energy. (Doing this will not release any of the love you feel for your family since the intention is to clear only that which is old and stuck.) Begin dancing around this baggage and, taking one item at a time, find a way to throw or kick this old energy into the volcano until it is all gone. Feel the joy of letting it go and becoming lighter and free.*

*Then feel all the inner baggage you hold from other sources such as friends, lovers, work colleagues, etc. and repeat the process. Have as much fun as possible and let yourself feel excited about releasing all this 'old stuff'.*

*When you are complete, ask the element of fire to transform this energy and send it to where it needs to go. Then begin to breathe in the element of fire and imagine this as an orange-red flow of energy entering your body. Allow it to fill all the places once occupied by the 'old energy'. Feel the power of fire in your veins and also in your heart and belly. Allow it to transform any remaining energy in your body that is not serving you. Take as much of this energy as you wish and when you are ready climb down from the summit, go back through the landscape and return to your body.*

*Notice if you feel any lighter or clearer. Repeat this exercise whenever you need to release stuck energy.*

# Power Animals

*Ask the wild bee what the Druids knew.*

Old English saying

There was a time when humanity felt it was a part of nature, and at such a time the physical and spiritual worlds overlapped and intermingled. Many indigenous peoples, including the Celts of Britain and the shamanic cultures of North and South America, connected and worked with the power or medicine of animal spirits. Legends still speak of these times, and all the strange and distorted stories about werewolves and vampires originate from these shamanic experiences with animal spirits. In ancient Celtic legends Taliesin, the great Druid shaman of Britain, was said to have had a great affinity with these beings and was credited with being able to shape-shift himself into any animal he wished. Every species of animal – both those that are around today and those that are now extinct – can be met in the spirit realms. Mythical beasts such as dragons and unicorns are very much present in these realms and are every bit as helpful and powerful as creatures such as horses, wolves or cats. Meeting a power animal guardian is not like meeting the individual consciousness of an animal but more like connecting with the spirit or essence of a whole species, and therefore these beings contain tremendous power and wisdom. Each spirit brings different gifts and the power of one is no better than that of another. The spirits are simply different, and are helpful or appropriate at different times. It is challenging for me to convey fully the power, wisdom and beauty of meeting and working with such beings since these experiences transcend words. Our language is so orientated to describing objective reality. Power animals walk with every human being and are able to guard our connection to the web and enhance and protect our energy. This important function of spirit was known to our ancestors but has now been almost universally forgotten. These beings soon lose interest in us if we are not open to their help and guidance or if we follow a lifestyle that does not honour the web of all things. According to shamanic wisdom, if these guides leave us then problems will begin to occur and we may experience power loss and the even more serious state of soul loss where bits of our consciousness begin to desert us because we are no longer a safe container for them. This leaves us in the sorry state of being open to energies that are inappropriate for our health and wellbeing. So it is important to honour and build our relationship with these guardians.

It is entirely possible to have several power animals working with us at any one time. Some will be more permanent companions, whereas others may come and go. According to Native American wisdom we usually have one guardian who permanently protects our Warrior side and another that permanently watches over our Priestess side. In work involving with such beings, and most of the beings that inhabit the Otherworld, it is they who choose us rather than the other way round, so allow for some pleasant surprises. A mouse may seem less glamorous than a wolf yet it is wise not to refuse its help because each power animal has many unique gifts and blessings to bestow. Although shamanic journeys are usually aided by the rhythmic sound of drumming or some other instrument such as the rattle, such journeys can also be made using recorded meditative or shamanic music.

## Meeting an Animal Guide

*Find time for an inner journey when you will not be disturbed, and begin to centre and connect with the cycle of breath. Open to feel your connection to the web of life.*

*Open your inner senses and imagine standing on the edge of a running stream. Feel your feet on the soft bank, hear the sound of the flowing stream as it passes over and around the rocks, smell the damp air and listen to the sounds of nature. When you are ready, cross over to the other side and begin to explore the landscape. Mentally call for your animal guide to join you. In this place you may meet many creatures – some may scamper off or avoid you, and others you may feel you want to avoid. Somewhere in this place is an animal guide that will not avoid you and you will not want to avoid, no matter what it looks like. This animal will usually be warm blooded and will feel friendly, although if a mythical creature appears then that is also fine. Just trust who turns up and allow yourself to be surprised. Be with this being and gaze softly into its eyes. Connect with this being and begin to feel the qualities this guide has – courage, stamina, strength, stealth, a strong instinct, or perhaps the ability to climb or run very fast.*

*Get a feel for its qualities and see what it wants to offer you, such as the resourcefulness of a fox, the keen vision of a cat, the determination of a wolf, the strength of a bear.*

*Ask your guide to take you on a journey to show you a place where you can find healing and rest. This may be in a circle of standing stones, a crystal cave, or perhaps a waterfall. In this place sit with your guide and allow this being to impart to you some of its qualities. Feel the power of this creature and breathe it in so that you can bring its gifts back to the physical world with you. If you wish, ask for permission to merge with this creature's energy, and if you get a 'yes' then imagine stepping into its form and looking out at the world through its eyes.*

*When you are ready, separate from your guide but go with it back the way you came, through the landscape to the stream. Here thank and leave your guide, cross over the stream and return to full waking consciousness.*

# Tree Spirits

Tree spirits are wonderful beings to connect with. Indigenous tribal peoples considered trees holy and sacred and doorways to other worlds. I have meditated with trees for many years and have found different species to be helpful at different times. If you want to connect with tree spirits go and seek them out in wild places, feel their presence and speak to them of what you would like help with in your life. Trust your intuition and pick only trees that give you a feeling of openness and inner stillness.

*Alder* – *This tree is a faerie tree and gives access to seekers who want to journey to the faerie realms. The spirit of this tree is protective and can awaken the courage and strength we need to move forward in the face of adversity. This tree is helpful in facing those things that have previously been avoided, and it helps to blend strength with generosity of spirit.*

*Apple* – *This is a tree of abundance, magic and immortality. It is connected to the fabled land of immortality, the Isle of Apples of Celtic mythology. Apples are a universal symbol of plenty and love. Aphrodite, the Greek goddess of love and beauty, had the apple as her symbol. The spirit of this tree can teach lessons about love and generosity, faith and gratitude.*

*Ash* – *In northern European mythology the ash is known as Yggdrasil, the Great World Tree that connects the three worlds of the gods and goddesses, humanity and the ancestors. The spirit of this tree can help to bring balance between the inner and the outer and to heal the loneliness of the human spirit. To the ancient Celts this tree was the guardian of the laws of the universe and thus represented order.*

**Aspen** – *The Irish Celts called the aspen the 'shield tree' because their warriors carried shields made of aspen into battle. The Celts believed the aspen could teach them how to overcome fear. By wearing a crown of aspen leaves legendary heroes in Greek mythology were granted the protection of the Goddess, who allowed them to enter the Underworld and return safely.*

**Birch** – *This is a tree of new beginnings, birth and springtime. The spirit of the birch can help to break new ground and it brings strength and protection in adversity. This is the tree most associated with the youthful aspect of the Goddess.*

**Elder** – *This tree is most associated with the waning moon and the waning year. It was said to be under the protection of the ancient Goddess and it was considered bad luck to cut one down with selfish intent. Throughout northern Europe this tree was linked to death and magic. The spirit of the elder teaches lessons about honour and dignity and also about death itself.*

**Hawthorn** – *The hawthorn is a faerie tree and represents love, fertility and sexual enjoyment. This is a tree of the heart and is helpful in healing any issue involving heartbreak, stress and fear. Sprigs of it can be given as an expression of love and friendship. This tree is associated with the Welsh goddess Blodeuwed.*

**Hazel** – *This tree is associated with communication, knowledge, healing, magic and understanding. It is the tree of poetry, which our ancestors regarded as the highest form of magic. The hazel is associated with the element of air, and hazel groves are highly charged with the magical energy of inspiration and exhilaration.*

**Holly** – *The holly is a tree with a strong masculine energy that has gifts of health and potent life force for those it favours. It can help awaken unconditional love and it can help in restoring inner balance. The lesson of this tree is similar to that of the Hanged Man tarot card, which teaches the virtue of personal sacrifice in order to attain something of greater value.*

**Oak** – *The oak was the tree most revered by the Welsh Druids. Its Celtic name translates as 'doorway'. It is generally seen as a masculine tree with associations to the energy of summer. The spirit of the oak can help those who sit with it to open the way to the qualities of courage, determination, endurance, faith and inner peace. King Arthur's table was reportedly made from a single slice of a giant oak, and Merlin weaved his magic with a wand made of oak.*

**Pine** – *The Druids burnt huge fires of pine and yew at the winter solstice to call back the sun from its time in the Underworld. The pine is a feminine tree and its spirit is helpful in cleansing negativity, yet it is also able to teach seekers how to become a spiritual warrior.*

**Rowan** – *This tree is said to bring physical and spiritual healing. It is also able to strengthen positive life-force energy and help to develop latent psychic abilities. Having a rowan tree near your house can help to ward off 'negative' influences. The berry has a pentagram, the ancient symbol of magical protection, at its base. This tree is sacred to the English goddess Brigantia and to Brigit of the Irish Celts.*

**Willow** – *The willow was known in Celtic folklore as a tree of enchantment and mystery. The spirit of this tree is connected to water and the moon, and it is a great ally when trying to reconnect to deeply buried emotions, intuition and the imagination. In ancient times poets, musicians and priestesses would sit in willow groves for inspiration.*

*Yew – The yew can live for as long as perhaps 3,000–4,000 years, and it has long been revered as a tree of death, regeneration and rebirth. This is a tree that reminds us of our links to the earth and to the ancestors of the land. Spending time in meditation with this tree can help with grief and loss and the fear of death or endings. The lesson of the yew is that death can be transcended.*

## The Angelic Presence

> *Every blade of grass has its Angel*
>
> *that bends over it and whispers, grow, grow.*

The Talmud

Angels appear in the cosmology of all the major religions of the world and have been described in many different cultures through imagery, poetry and stories. In the West we seem to be experiencing a great wave of angels who are reaching out through the dimensions to touch us. They appeared to many shamans and mystics for thousands of years and then went on to appear in biblical times, and then again during the medieval period. The recent wave of contact began as far back as the eighteenth century, and now these angelic beings are gathering in strength as they prepare to assist in the great change as we pass from the Age of Pisces to the Age of Aquarius.

Angels have been messengers in the Jewish, Christian and Islamic traditions. Angels are an important part of the Kabbala, a tradition of Jewish mysticism, where each sephiroth or level has its own angel. The Archangel Gabriel appeared at the time of the birth of Jesus, and also came to Mohammed to dictate the Koran.

The angelic presence has been portrayed in the works of art of the great masters such as Rembrandt, and the Pre-Raphaelites, and has also appeared in the written works of Dante, John Milton and William Blake. Madame Blavatsky, the founder of the Theosophical

Movement, and the mystic Rudolf Steiner both wrote extensively on angels and their role in human affairs.

Nowadays they appear everywhere: in art, music, films, TV programmes, newspaper articles and books. Although traditionally these beings have been portrayed as male, they are androgynous and can adopt the appearance of either gender. As light beings, angels are on a very separate evolutionary path from humanity, the path of pure service. This means that angels do not have free will as we do and so are unable to make choices that separate them from the web of all things. They are the servers of the Spirit of All Things, and their presence amongst us can have the beneficial effect of purifying our energy, raising our consciousness and opening us to impulses of divine inspiration. Humanity is a channel through which the angelic presence can work, especially in the fields of creativity, healing (including the healing of the earth), technology and miracles. One of the principles that seems to apply when working with angels is that they respond to calls from the heart, not to the desperate pleas of the negative ego. Requests for help have a better chance of being heard if they come from a calm, sincere and centred space. The angelic presence is then able, with our permission, to enter our reality and help us to advance on our path of evolution. More than any other group of helpers angels work with synchronicity and miracles. Problems that seem unsolvable can be resolved with the assistance of these beings. Again, our particular belief system affects the degree of contact or help allowed in. Starting to believe in angels does not mean that suddenly we must become naive or simple minded; rather, it means we expand what we consider possible.

Every soul quality that can be conceived of – creativity, fun, freedom, bliss, sacred sexuality, harmony, wisdom – has an angel consciousness that holds the blueprint of that quality. There are angels that oversee the elementals in the physical, emotional and mental realms too – the 'greater builders' that direct the work of the 'lesser builders'. Angels oversee the elementals that work to produce sound, colour, money, rain, snow and sunshine. Everything that can be conceived of has an angel that holds the blueprint for its existence. Some angels have yet to awaken and come into existence, such as the angel of a project not yet thought of, the angel of an invention yet to be imagined, or the angel of a healing path not yet revealed. There are angels of light that guide our way along the spiritual path as well as angels that hold the blueprint for such things as violence, chaos, fear and anger. Such 'dark' angels are not evil but exist simply to ensure that the process of growth continues, and they will remain here for as long as humanity needs them. Angelic helpers can perform psychic surgery when required and they are able to help us dissolve the old vows of other lifetimes that bind us to celibacy, poverty, suffering and obedience.

The angelic hierarchy includes those beings known as archangels, which have long been known to the Christian and Islamic traditions. These beings are not the exclusive property of any religious path for their task is to oversee the work of the 'greater builders' as well as to work directly with many groups of light workers across the world. Since much of my spiritual growth has come through shamanism and magic I was initially unsure about working with angels or archangels, but I soon changed my mind after being touched and helped by them.

## The Archangels

*One method to connect with these beings in meditation is to face the direction associated with the angel and then visualise a doorway covered with a curtain of the associated colour. Mentally call to the being and pull back the curtain to reveal a landscape. Step into the landscape and meet the archangel. Invite this being to help you and open to its help in any way it comes.*

**Raphael** *is connected to the direction of the east, the element of air and the colours yellow and gold. This being works with issues of communication, creativity, healing and the mental realm. Raphael is the great healer angel.*

**Michael** *is connected to the south, the element of fire and the colour golden red. Michael is the archangel of the sun and works with issues of balance, boundaries, courage, faith, power and protection. Michael is the spiritual Warrior.*

**Gabriel** *is connected to the west, the element of water and the colours blue and sea-green. Gabriel is the archangel of the moon and works with beauty, dreams, harmony, hope, visions, love and the emotional realm. Gabriel is the messenger.*

**Auriel** *is connected to the north, the element of earth and the colours of black and earth brown. Auriel is the archangel of the physical earth and works with the faerie realm, forgiveness, silence, wisdom and all things physical. Auriel is the angel of the mysteries.*

## Angels of Violet Fire for Purification

*Connect with your cycle of breath and imagine breathing in a beautiful violet-white light. Breathe this light into your auric field and allow yourself to feel the light spiralling around you. Then imagine breathing into existence a crown of violet-white light that begins to spiral around your head. Feel the peace and expansiveness that this light brings. Feel this crown being drawn down like a curtain around you, surrounding you with a violet-white mist. When you step through the mist you will find a golden staircase leading up into the heavens. Begin to ascend the staircase and leave the world far below until you come to a doorway that appears tinged with a violet fire. On the other side of this doorway* are the Angels of the Violet Fire who can help you in cleansing and purifying your auric field. Step through this doorway and allow a new ethereal landscape to rise up around you. In this landscape call to the Angels of Violet Fire to surround you. Just wait for these beings to appear. They bring a violet light that begins to sweep through and around you. This light gets stronger and stronger until it bursts into a violet flame. All negativity is purged in this flame. Allow this light to reach deep into your psyche, releasing you at a cellular, emotional and mental level.

Stay here with these beautiful beings for as long as you wish then thank them and return the way you came. Go back through the door, down the staircase and through the mist to return to your body.

## Solar Angels for Spiritual Transformation

Connect with your cycle of breath and imagine breathing the golden light of the sun into your body. Breathe this light into your auric field and allow it to spiral around you. Then imagine that you can breathe into existence a crown of golden white light that begins to spiral around your head. Feel the power of this light and allow it to form a golden-white mist around you. Draw down this light so that it forms a mist of golden light around you. When you step through this mist you find a bright golden staircase leading up into the heavens. Begin to ascend the staircase until you come to a doorway tinged with bright golden fire. On the other side of this doorway are solar angels that can assist in your path of transformation. Step through this doorway and allow a new ethereal landscape to rise up around you. Then simply call to the Angels of Solar Light to surround you and wait for them to arrive. These beings bring with them the power of the sun and they begin to send to you a gentle golden light that sweeps through and

*around you. This light reaches into the very cells of your body and
into your very DNA, the blueprint of the physical body. In this
light surrender any negativity that you hold and allow it to be
taken away. This light will eventually begin to work on
transforming the structure of your DNA at an etheric level. Just
ask for this to happen and allow these beings to create a new DNA
structure for you. This will help unblock many of the hidden
abilities that lie dormant within you. Allow this light to flow into
your auric field, making it stronger and healing any rips and tears
in its outer shell. Become bathed in a gentle golden light.*

*Stay here for as long as you wish then thank these beings and
return the way you came, back through the door, down the
staircase and through the mist to your body.*

# 8 CONSCIOUS MANIFESTING

*The greatest achievement was at first, and for a time a dream.*

*The oak sleeps in the acorn; the bird waits in the egg,*

*And in the highest vision of the soul a waking angel stirs.*

*Dreams are the seedlings of reality.*

James Allen

## Magic and Manifesting

Manifesting is the natural and magical function of our consciousness that opens us to the pure potentiality of our being. On a day-to-day basis it is the Basic Self, ideally under the awareness, guidance and direction of the Conscious Self, that generates our personal reality. This happens when the Conscious Self is aware of the relationship between the inner and the outer realities. However, for the most part the collective consciousness of humanity is now very much within the paradigm of logic and rational thinking, and magic is generally seen as something belonging to the primitive or childish mind. For thousands of years our ancestors felt connected to the web of life and knew that magic was as natural as the sun rising each day. Our consciousness is naturally seated within the web of life, despite our best efforts to separate ourselves, and when we know this we will know magic. The magical power of the web is vast and deep for it is the same power that grows a leaf and holds the planets in their orbit around the sun. Manifesting is the art of changing consciousness at will and using it to weave the unseen into the seen. It is an ancient art and the ultimate adventure of working with the power of consciousness and spirit to create a heaven on earth. Working with this power requires responsibility and integrity – magic cannot be employed for 'get rich quick' schemes nor can it be used to violate another individual's chosen life path without unhappy consequences. Many people are becoming interested in the possibility that magic really does exist, and when enough people change their beliefs concerning what is possible the world we live in will change. As more and more people consciously begin to generate realities that are abundant, flowing, joyful and loving, less energy will be expended on sustaining old, limiting thought forms and belief systems about the nature of reality.

In order to understand fully our inner potential and grow it is essential to learn the process of conscious manifesting, in which a consciousness is focused on generating what is wanted and needed on the physical plane. There are many different ways of doing this and in this chapter I will outline just a few techniques that can work very well.

Manifesting is a wonderful way to grow because everything we manifest brings with it a basket full of gifts of growth. The creation of this book was a manifestation process: I had the idea, did the inner work and, hey presto, a publisher very shortly afterwards contacted me and asked me if I wanted to write a book – and this was before I had written a single word or approached anyone about it. Writing the book was also a manifestation process, one that gave me many wonderful gifts and interesting challenges. For one thing I came face to face with much of my internal resistance to graceful success.

It is fine and ethical to use magic to attract more love into your life yet it is a violation to use it to try to make a certain individual fall in love with you. A good friend of mine who was having problems in her marriage took her husband along to a manifesting workshop. They each went through a process of clarifying and working on manifesting what they wanted. At the end of the workshop my friend asked her husband what he had wanted to manifest and he replied that he had worked on manifesting her falling back in love with him. She was furious and thought he was trying to manipulate her feelings. A few months later they separated and eventually divorced. In the workshop my friend had worked on bringing more love and joy into her life, and now she has considerably more of both, whereas her ex-husband went through a very difficult time emotionally for several months.

The power inherent in the web can be called upon for both 'positive' and 'negative' purposes – like electricity can both light a house or badly burn someone. Whatever is sent out will eventually return along the strands of the web, and so if healing and love are sent these will return, if ill-will and hatred are sent that is what will return in equal measure. People who work with magic tend not to be fools and are usually aware that each act carries certain consequences. It is wise to use magic to uplift yourself as well as others.

We come into the physical world to learn how to engage and interact with it, and to weave into it the dreams of our heart. Therefore we cannot learn or grow very much when we seek to escape this world. Manifestation is a way to connect with the world and with the spiritual dimensions in a meaningful way. Conscious manifestation takes our innermost wishes, dreams and desires and turns them into physical form around us. Manifestation is a path of growth that can become a juicy experience when it involves creating a life that works in every area. Can you picture all your relationships being loving and joyful, your physical body being radiantly healthy, your work life being joyful, creative and richly rewarded? Can you imagine having enough money to provide all you want and need in the world?

## Levels of Manifesting

*Reality is created through:*
◆ *the beliefs we hold*

◆ *the thoughts and emotions they produce*

◆ *the choices we make*

◆ *the words and actions we engage with*

◆ *our ability to imagine and focus*

◆ *our levels of commitment and perseverance*

◆ *our expectations*

◆ *our levels of self-awareness, trusting in spirit, self-love and self-esteem*

Manifesting is a natural phenomenon of the universe and it is useful to know when the tides are in our favour. The cycles of the moon have a strong influence on manifesting because the moon affects both our emotional and physical bodies.

## The Cycles of the Moon

**The New Moon** – *A good time to give birth to new projects, beginnings, directions and intentions, as well as a good time to make decisions. Contemplate your dreams and visions.*

**The Waxing Moon** – *A time for growth and the energising of all new ideas. This period is a good time for manifesting.*

**The Full Moon** – *A time for celebration, culmination, fruition and completion. This is the best time for manifesting since the moon is full with power.*

**The Waning Moon** – *A time to release the old on all levels, and to clear any internal or external clutter.*

**The Dark Moon** – *A good time for inner reflection, inner stillness, looking at shadow issues, transformation and the assimilation of wisdom on all levels.*

# Three Manifesting Processes

The three processes outlined here can all work well, yet the first two may work better if you have no deep-rooted blocks to having what you want. If what you want is just beyond your reach at present use either process one or two. If you feel it lies beyond the horizon of probability use process three.

## *Process One*

### *Engage Your Chakras*

*The first step is to be clear on what it is you want. Then translate that into an image. If you want more joy, perhaps see this as a radiant sun; if you want more peace, perhaps see this as a tranquil lake. If you want a specific job choose an image such as a computer terminal or a pen or toolbox. With this image meditate on each chakra, starting at the base and completing with the crown. Move on to the next chakra when you feel ready. This exercise uses the seven chakras in the body and does not include the Star and Earth chakras.*

*The meditation itself involves two parts: for the first part focus on the symbol for ten minutes and feel the energy of it; for the second part imagine placing the symbol in a chakra and then opening to feel its power radiating through your body. The exception to this is on day seven when you imagine releasing the symbol to spirit through your Crown Chakra and seeing it being placed in a stellar web of light.*

*Day One – Place the symbol within the raw life-force energy that is found in your base. Bathe the symbol in the colour red of this chakra.*

**Day Two** – *Place the symbol in your centre of pleasure and bathe it in the colour orange of this chakra.*

**Day Three** – *Place the symbol in your radiant power centre and feel it radiating its power to your bright will in order to manifest what you want. Bathe it in the colour yellow of this chakra.*

**Day Four** – *Place your symbol in your centre of love. Bathe it in the colour green of this chakra.*

**Day Five** – *Place the symbol in your centre of self-expression. Bathe it in the colour light-blue of this chakra.*

**Day Six** – *Place the symbol in your centre of vision. Bathe it in the colour deep-blue of this chakra.*

**Day Seven** – *Place the symbol in your crown centre, which is your personal gateway to spirit. Bathe it in the colours of amethyst and white of this chakra before letting it go and seeing it merge with the web of all things. See it sending light out into the cosmos and surrender your dream to the universe and let it go.*

*Process Two*

## Manifesting With the Elements

*For this process each day sit and face the direction of one element. Attune to this element and ask for its help. Starting in the east with air and ending in the centre with spirit, spend some time meditating with each direction and only move on to the next when you feel complete in that direction. It can help if you find an object that represents the direction, such as a feather for air, a candle for fire, a chalice for water or a crystal for earth. Place the object in front of you as you meditate. It helps if you actually face the direction you are working with. This can be done by orientating yourself to the directions of the rising and setting sun.*

*Air – Begin with east, the element of the mind. This is the place of spring, innocence, inspiration and birth. In meditation imagine inviting this element into your manifesting process. Visualise this direction as a blue sky with a sun rising. Feel the power and freshness of the wind on your face.*

*Spend time meditating on what you want to manifest in the world. Ask for inspiration and clarity. Begin to stand in the realm of possibility and believe that in the east nothing is impossible. Feel the sun rising on your dreams.*

*Fire – When you are ready move to the direction of south, the element of the will. This is the place of summer, faith, relationships, strength and sexuality. Visualise this direction as a radiant sun high in the heavens.*

*In meditation sit with this element and activate your will to manifest what you want. Feel courage, passion and enthusiasm for what you want. Allow this to build up like a fire within you.*

*Water – When you are ready turn to the direction of west, the element of the emotions. This is the place of love, maturity, introspection and dreams. Visualise this direction as a vast and powerful ocean.*

*Spend time meditating on having what you want. Imagine the joy and happiness you will feel when you have it and build a wave of emotion that can flow out into the world and attract what you want.*

*Earth – When you are ready turn to the direction of north, the element of all things physical. This is the place of age, patience, prosperity, ritual, teaching and wisdom. Visualise this direction as a forest surrounding a great mountain. Spend time beginning to focus on the practical steps you need to take to actualise your dream and also the structures you will need to build to support it.*

> **Spirit** – *When you are ready turn to the centre, the element of ether or prana or life-force energy. This is the place of transformation and rebirth. Visualise this direction as the centre of a great spiralling galaxy or the centre of a large Celtic labyrinth.*
>
> *In this place imagine that you can surrender your dream to spirit. Let go of your visions and send them out into the universe. Dwell here on the qualities of gratitude and trust and being open to receive. Then expect the best to happen.*

## Process Three

### STEP ONE – OPEN TO THE POWER OF THE PRIESTESS

> *Every creative act involves a new innocence of perception, liberated from the cataract of accepted belief.*
>
> Arthur Koestler

Manifesting is like placing a seed in fertile ground and waiting for rain and sunlight to bring it forth. The seed of all our dreams and highest visions can be found within the heart, and these dreams are ever unfolding and expanding beyond present horizons. As we follow our dreams with courage and perseverance, life will never be the same again. Our highest visions, once liberated from the heart, can lead us on an adventurous tour towards the impossible and out the other side to the possible and the probable. We will know our vision by the degree of passion we feel for it, for when an idea or inspiration comes along and we feel absolutely no passion for it then it has no energy behind it to manifest in the world. Knowing what we want is crucial in beginning to waken to new possibilities for living life to the full. It is only through awakening or creating a dream of how we want to be in life that we gain enough velocity to break through the boundaries of fear and limitation that have been woven about us by the False Self. We all have many childlike and joyful yearnings that sleep like children within our hearts and these sleeping yearnings hold many keys for the future. Growing up, many of us have cast aside our dreams as we would old and broken toys, yet they still exist within sleeping. As we grew, other dreams were born and these too perhaps we cast aside as unrealistic and unobtainable. Many of us know but have forgotten the role that fun, play and imagination has in shaping our world. We have become serious and realistic grown-ups and magic does not always exist alongside such seriousness. As children we lived within the rich and vibrant world of the imagination yet this did not make us psychotic individuals who were unable to interact with the world – on the contrary, it made interaction with the world rich and pleasurable. Imagination is a gateway to the dreams of the soul and these can become like golden arrows that propel us through the known to the landscapes of the greater beyond.

Marissa was in her late thirties and at a crossroads in her life. Some friends were running a vision quest (from the North American native tradition) that involved going out in nature in order to get a vision or answer to a problem from spirit, and she decided to take part. She fasted for a day and then went out into Ashdown Forest to spend some time alone with nature. She created a medicine wheel within the trees and sat there and watched the sun move slowly across the bright heavens. She took time to pray and meditate and eventually, just before her time in nature was coming to an end, she received a vision of giving a talk in front of a large and appreciative audience. She was a little amazed and excited for she had no public speaking experience, yet she decided to follow her vision and within a year had begun to give talks and run workshops on spirituality. She went on a few years later to run many successful retreats on spirituality and magic in Britain and America.

Step One is about accessing the vision of the Priestess, so allow plenty of time and space for yourself to find the dream of your heart. It can be helpful to spend time alone, perhaps going for long, slow walks in nature or taking the time to enjoy long, luxurious, hot baths. Stop being busy and slow down to allow the vision of the Priestess to open. Open to the chaos of pure creativity and commit to spending some time each day contemplating what is it you truly want.

A good friend of mine, Nick Williams, a writer and founder of the Heart at Work project, worked for a number of years in marketing and sales and by his late twenties was financially successful. Despite his success he became disillusioned and wondered why. One day he sat down and asked himself the question 'So what would I really like to do?' and the answer that came was 'to teach, inspire, contribute, write, travel and communicate'. For several years he resisted the pull of his intuition and laid aside his dream. Nick says, 'Eventually I began to realise that my intuition was not my enemy but my guide, so I plucked up courage and quit the corporate world. Over the subsequent 12 years I have created the life I really dreamed of. I have written books, travelled to many different countries to teach, and built a successful business, all because I listened to and followed my dreams.'

## Write Down Your Dreams

From a blank piece of A4 paper cut out a large egg shape. On it write down everything that you would like to show up in your life in the near future. Include the possible, the probable and the impossible. Do not limit yourself. Write for a while with your dominant hand and then change to see how it is to write down your dreams with your non-dominant hand. Include the essence of what you want – such as happiness, joy and inner peace – and also include the tangible things you want – such as to live closer to nature, to have a deeper and more intimate relationship with your partner, to have a new job in a new exciting town. If you are writing in neat orderly lines try writing in a chaotic fashion across the page or in a spiral.

Continue until you feel you are finished. Keep this sheet and put it on a wall where you can read it often to remind you of what you want to create in your life. (You may want to put it in a space away from any critical or doubting individuals.)

Practise writing down your dreams on a regular basis, perhaps once a month or once every few months, and do not worry about repeating what you want to manifest.

## A Collage of Dreams

Find a large sheet of paper or card and write at the top your name and the date.

Collect a large number of images from magazines, postcards, travel brochures, etc. Begin to scan through them and cut out those images that speak to you – that is, that give you a sense of joy, peace or passion, or whatever it is you want more of in your life. Collect as many images as you can and be clear on what each one represents. So a picture of a flamenco dancer may represent passion to you, a leaping stag may represent faith, a rosebud a new project, a star success in an interview, and so on. When you are ready begin to paste each image on to your paper and make a beautiful collage of what you want to invite into your life. Feel the excitement of having all of these things and qualities in your life.

Keep adding images until the collage is finished. Take as long as you wish and even when you feel it is complete you can always add more images later if you wish. Hang your collage in a place where you can see it each day. If you put it in your bedroom you can see the collage as you are waking up or going to sleep.

## STEP TWO – ENROL THE SUPPORT OF YOUR BASIC SELF

Begin this step only when you are clear what it is you want to create in the world. This may be a good time to review some of the exercises in Chapter 3 regarding the Basic Self. The Basic Self is able to influence the elemental builders of form and so doing these exercises will automatically alter the way these beings work for you in your life.

### Your Beliefs

Are they expansive or are they limiting? Work on finding beliefs that block the appearance in the world of what you want and then change them. What beliefs would be supportive of your dreams and help them manifest in the world? This is a good time to review Chapter 4, particularly the sections How to Find Our Beliefs and Changing Beliefs.

## *Check Your Beliefs*

*How possible do you feel it is to have what you want to manifest?*

*Do you believe there are enough resources and opportunities to go round?*

*Do you feel you deserve to have what you want?*

*What do you believe is preventing you from having what you want?*

*Look at how you feel about issues such as luck, fate or karma, competition, disappointment, failure, win/lose scenarios.*

### Release the Baggage of the Past

Use the meditation from Chapter 7 called Inner Cleansing with Fire to release any clutter and baggage the Basic Self is holding that prevents you from creating what you want. Check that you have released any guilt or a feeling that you do not deserve what you want. Let go of old disappointment or upset that could be blocking the way.

Letting go of the old makes way for the new. This is very much like the process of weeding before the planting of new seeds.

## Engage Your Emotions

Check the enthusiasm and passion your Basic Self holds for what you want. Feel all your desire for what you want and do not feel bad about feeling desire. There has been much misinformation about desire on the spiritual path; desire has been labelled wrong and this itself has been the cause of much suffering. Without the passion of the Basic Self life can only be half lived. Fully engage your passion for what you want and temper desire with the detachment of the Conscious Self. Awaken your love for life and for what you want. Love is the most powerful force in the universe so evoke it from within, fill yourself with this power and pour it out towards what you want.

## Train Your Senses

Begin to train your senses to notice the things you want to manifest in your life. Practise turning away from the things you do not want in your life – as if you are turning off a light switch – and begin to direct your senses towards what you want. If you want to manifest more joy then begin to watch out for joy in the world. If you want to manifest more love then notice the love that is expressed around you. Practise noticing people in the street who seem to hold the quality you are seeking to manifest. Find out where such people hang out. Scan magazines for snippets of what you are seeking. Go and see films or plays that hold elements of what you are looking for.

Surround yourself with things that can impact on your senses and remind you of what you want to manifest. If it is love, try listening to music that opens your heart; if it is inner peace, perhaps have an image such as a statuette of the Buddha in your home; if it is abundance, perhaps wear something that opens you to feel that the world is an abundant place for you. I have collected over the last few years a number of watches in different colours and styles, and to each one I have assigned a different meaning – something that I want to manifest in my life. Now whenever I check the time my Basic Self is reminded of that particular aim.

## Use Your Memory

Ask your Basic Self to send you memories of the times when you had what you wanted. Remember the feelings of joy and empowerment from your past. Your Basic Self can give you memories of having what you wanted in other lifetimes too. There may also be memories of times when you did not have what you wanted and these may be blocking you, so ask that these become visible so they can be transformed. If your Basic Self presents such a memory simply accept it and then in your mind's eye see the memory as a still photograph, draw a red cross through it and see yourself ripping the image into many pieces and then burning them. This is a communication to your Basic Self to release this old memory.

## Employ Ritual

The Basic Self loves ritual and its attention is grabbed through sensory information such as the flickering of a candle flame, the smell of burning incense, the chiming of bells and Tibetan singing bowls, the sound of rhythmic drumming or chanting, the glow of a brightly burning fire, or anything it perceives to be out of the ordinary.

In designing a ritual be aware of having a clear beginning and end. The content of a ritual needs to have a clearly defined purpose, such as releasing or invoking something. In working with ritual be as creative as possible and have lots of fun. Do not worry about getting anything wrong and remember that the Basic Self loves to have fun and is attracted by laughter. Many magical traditions employ ritual, which usually takes the form of creating sacred space, invoking the five elements and building a circle of power. Some schools use the archangels instead of the elements, but both work very well.

Ritual can be carried out alone or in a group, it can be based on a tradition such as Wicca, Tantra or Shamanism, or it can be made up. It is unfortunately beyond the scope of this book to describe all the varied ways that ritual can be used for manifesting. Just be creative!

### Step Three – engage the power of the Warrior

> *Bless the present.*
>
> *Trust Yourself.*
>
> *Expect the Best.*
>
> Serge Kahili King

### Put Your Will in Gear

The personal will is our unique and personal drive to achieve what we want. This is the driving force behind the Warrior. The ethical use of the will always leads to win/win scenarios. How will what you want benefit others also? When engaging your will check that you are benefiting the planet as well as yourself. Use the will only for win/win situations and never to harm another intentionally.

## The Power of Intention

*Desire leads to wanting something and becoming very attached to things happening or working out in a certain way. Desire is held within the Basic Self and intention is an attribute of the Conscious Self. Intention and desire both lead to wanting something but intention differs in that there is no attachment to how and when it comes. With intention, it is like making a choice and then trusting that the universe will bring you what you want in the way that is perfect for where you are in your life.*

*Desire is where a certain person must love you or a situation must turn out in a certain way. This is one sure way to eventually experience disappointment and pain.*

*Feel the desire for something to happen and then consciously apply the power of intention, which is pure desire without attachment. Pure intention does not require people to act as you would wish them to, nor does it require things to turn out exactly according to some specified plan.*

## Choices

Are they well or ill informed? Gather as much information as possible from your inner world through the Priestess, and also from the outer world through the Warrior. Meditate on the choices before you and always choose the path that feels lightest in your body. Be aware of making choices based on what you think other people want. Review the exercise in Chapter 1 called Choose Joy.

## Focus

Begin to focus on what you want rather than what you do not want. This takes practice because often our conscious mind has been taught to look out for what is wrong in life in order to either avoid or fix it. Our conscious mind then looks out into our reality for the things that are wrong with it. Changing your focus means turning away from the things that are not working and putting your mental and emotional energy into what you want more of. What you dwell on will increase in your life. Practise awareness and notice whenever you are dwelling on the things you do not want. When this happens simply make a conscious effort to bring to mind something you want more of in your life. If there is something burning in your mind that needs resolving then work on this and then return to focusing on what you want. Let nothing distract you from your goals.

## *Thoughts*

Do you generate loving or fearful thoughts about having what you want? Are your thoughts about lack or abundance? What is the most loving or joyful thought that you can hold about manifesting what you want?

Spend time each day dwelling on thoughts of appreciation and gratitude for the things that you have already invited into your life. Gratitude is a very powerful quality when it comes to manifesting. If you want more happiness then feel gratitude for the glimmers of happiness already in your life and very soon you will have a roaring fire. Feel grateful for the happiness that is flowing across the world in every moment. Whenever you notice people being happy practise being grateful for the gift they are offering you.

## *Imagination*

Imagine that you already have what you want and step into the feelings that having this thing or situation would evoke. Begin to expect the best to happen through the doorway of your imagination and be as creative as you can. Take time to play with the imagination and visualise what you would like to manifest in your life.

Ask yourself 'What is the most wonderful thing that could happen in this area of my life?' Suspend disbelief, put aside any worries about being disappointed and simply play with your imagination. Use your imagination rather like artists do when they paint a picture.

When playing with the imagination notice your level of passion for having what you want. If you want a specific quality – happiness, say – imagine how this quality could come into every area of your life, such as with family and friends and in meditation. If you want a specific job imagine that you now have that job and see how it feels. You may find that when you step into the energy of what you want and play with it for a while, you no longer really want it.

## Visualise What You Want

*Have what you want in mind and now begin to play with the imagination. If you want more money in your life go within and spend time fantasising about having more money. Imagine perhaps going on an amazing shopping spree or visiting an island where there is unlimited abundance and everything you ever wanted or desired is available. Visualise all the things you would do and, most importantly, step into how it would feel to be wealthy. Enjoy the feeling of being wealthy and bring the feeling of wealth back with you into your outer world. If you want more joy in your life imagine doing all the things that you think would bring you joy. If one of them is going on a wonderful holiday, imagine sitting on a beautiful beach having fun with friends. If another is doing something exciting like water skiing or hang gliding, imagine yourself there and feel the thrill of it. Again, it is the feeling that is important and that needs to be brought back into the outer world.*

*If you want more romantic love in your life, imagine being with a partner who absolutely adores you. Perhaps visualise having a moonlit stroll along a beautiful beach and making love in a beautiful and exotic place. Perhaps imagine you have many wonderful and supportive friends. Again, concentrate on the feeling that the imagery evokes and allow it to come back with you and be anchored in the world.*

*Play with visualisation and do not limit what is possible.*

### Words (spoken and written)

Are your words an expression of what you want to manifest or a negation of it? Are they an invitation or a rejection of what you want?

Notice whether the words you speak support what you want to create. Notice too how your words impact on your Basic Self and on your physical and emotional selves. Notice which words bring you down and which ones lift you up. Some words – such as should, must, try, impossible and evil – may have a restrictive effect on the Basic Self. Say 'yes' and 'no' consciously. Learn the skill of knowing when to speak to others about your dream and when to stay silent.

## Actions

Do your actions lead to manifesting what you want or are they taking you in the opposite direction? Are they in accordance with your inner guidance? Engage all your energy into moving towards what you want. If one route of action is blocked, be creative and discover another. Tune into your Priestess and know when it is appropriate to take small achievable steps and when it is time to take large leaps of faith. Be guided by the Inner Priestess and engage your Warrior Self. If you want to attract more love in your life, what are the ways you can begin to take action and give love to others? If you want to attract generosity from the universe, how can you begin to practise being generous? What actions can you take today that will send empowering ripples throughout the web? Every action leads to some sort of reaction, so ensure your every action is uplifting. Start to give what you most want to receive, yet avoid going over the top and tipping into sacrifice. Give only when you feel good in giving.

## Expect the Best

Begin to see your expected outcome as if it has happened. How would you feel if you had what you wanted? The feeling of high expectation can act like a magnet to attract your desired outcome. Check whether you feel you are beginning to open to the possibility that the best can happen. High expectation is a feeling of excitement that ripples through the physical and emotional bodies. How excited are you about what you want to manifest?

## Act As If

*Act as if you had what you wanted. If you want money, how could you enter into the feeling of wealth? Is there some small thing that you could buy that would make you feel very wealthy? The item does not have to be expensive yet it might get you into the feeling of wealth. If you want more joy, how could you get into the energy of feeling joyful now? Do not wait for joy to come – act as if you already had it. As a joyful person what would you do? Can you start doing those things now? Perhaps arrange to go to the theatre with some friends or throw a surprise party. If you want to allow change in your life then begin to act differently. Do something unexpected and see how it feels.*

## The Power of the Warrior

*In the morning face the rising sun and imagine that with each in-breath you can absorb pure sunlight. Imagine drawing this golden light into your solar plexus until it becomes so full that it feels as if a sun is being born in your belly. Continue to take in pure sunlight with each breath so that this inner sun begins to grow and radiate sunlight. Allow this radiating sun to pulse light and energy throughout your body with each beat of your heart. Discover what it is like to be a radiating sun. Feel the tremendous power in this light and imagine that you have the power to send this light to your dreams. See all of your bright visions of the future empowered with golden solar light.*

*When you are ready, slowly return to full waking consciousness. Notice how much more powerful you feel. Repeat this exercise as often as you wish.*

## Step Four – connect with the Unseen Friends

> *Ask, and it shall be given you;*
>
> *seek, and ye shall find;*
>
> *knock, and it shall be opened unto you.*
>
> Gospel of Matthew

Now is the time to connect with the community of light beings and your Higher Self. There is an abundance of help within the web and within your own consciousness. Call for help and open the way for miracles to happen. The power that sustains the universe is able to help you realise your dreams, for you contain the power of the whole web within. The Spirit of All Things is on your side and wants your life to be a heaven on earth – if you also desire it to be so. Begin to call on the help of the unseen friends and the Spirit of All Things through prayer or meditation. Call upon the archangels and surrender your dream to them. Journey with power animals to find a teacher in the inner world and hand this master your dream. Attune with nature spirits and elemental beings and ask for help.

## Step Five – surrender to the process

This step sounds simple and yet for some it can prove the most difficult. Step into the field of all possibilities and let your dream go. Release your dream to the forces of creation and stay detached from the outcome. Being attached to something blocks this process and so the trick is to intend something and then let go of it. Attachment leads to desperation, and there is nothing better than desperation for repelling what you want. The underlying energy of desperation is the feeling that you must have this thing in order to be happy or feel good enough. This is rooted in the belief that you are not good enough already. In order to engage fully your inner power it is necessary to utilise desire and release attachment. Letting go is like planting seeds in the earth and then simply forgetting about them. Not letting go is like planting seeds and then digging them up to check on their progress.

Manifesting is a wonderful learning process and there are no right and wrong ways to go about it. There are many different manifestation processes and they can all work very well, yet you may feel that you need to adapt and change them to your own temperament – and that is absolutely fine. Be creative and have lots of fun with these processes. Happy manifesting!

# 9 A TIME FOR SPIRITUAL GROWTH

*Focused, determined, enlightened public opinion*

*is the most potent force in the world.*

Alice Bailey

## Spirituality in the Twenty-First Century

It is apparent to many people living in the modern world that life is changing with increasing speed. The planet is now going through an age of transition and a great birthing process, the fruition of which we may not see in our lifetimes. The Age of Pisces (started with the birth of Jesus some 2,000 years ago) is coming to an end, and the energy of the next age, the Age of Aquarius, is already present. This means the next few decades will be a very powerful and exciting time to be alive. No age is better than another and each represents a stepping-stone on humanity's collective path of evolution. The Age of Pisces has been about love, devotion, service through sacrifice, suffering, martyrdom, the individual rather than the community, the formation of different religions and conflict through religious war. On the other hand, the Age of Aquarius (which will last for the next 2,000 years) will bring considerable reform and liberation from the old Piscean structures, for Aquarius signifies interdependence, community, co-operation between groups, and co-creation between nature, spirit and humanity. This age will see new energies becoming available in every sphere of life. Consequently synchronicity will seem more commonplace, life will have a greater sense of flow and the tremendous potential of consciousness will be more deeply understood and appreciated.

Now is a great time of initiation, and currently a major shift in consciousness is taking place. This is producing an explosion of interest in different kinds of spirituality, and many of us are looking at issues such as health and the environment from a more holistic perspective and re-evaluating our lifestyles – from how we relate to each other to how we work.

The many emerging forms of spirituality will help to break the stranglehold created by religious dogma and encourage a personal and mystical relationship with spirit. Religion has tended to teach that any relationship with spirit or the Divine can come about only via some kind of religious hierarchy. With the advent of Aquarius this will change and more and more people will be willing to create their own paths of devotion and spirituality and let go of ways of thinking that are based in fear. As we invite spirit into our lives the indwelling soul, which is but a spark in the consciousness of the Spirit of All Things, can begin to pulse its light through our physical, etheric, emotional and mental bodies – and this is when the process of releasing and transforming the entanglements of fear begins.

In Aquarius our Higher Selves will sound a collective note to call the attention of our Personality Selves away from the world of matter to embrace the realms of light and spirit. Spirituality is a path of the heart, opening us to unconditional love that cannot be adequately spoken about, only experienced. We are presently in a wonderful time of ascension, with all the kingdoms of nature, the planet itself and the human kingdom being uplifted. The path of ascension for humanity is one where the collective consciousness steadily shifts its centre from the Solar Plexus Chakra (with its issues about fear and the negative ego) to the more community-orientated Heart Chakra. Within Pisces, we have more or less fully explored the consequences of conflict, fear, struggle and suffering, and now we are ready to step beyond these limiting ways of being with each other and collectively step into the Heart or fourth Chakra. Some people refer to this process as going from a third-dimensional consciousness to a fourth-dimensional consciousness, and as this happens we will feel a pull from within to shift our beliefs, thoughts and choices. Everything is being given a boost and transformed with the new frequencies of light being made available. This will cause many old dark collective patterns to rise up and rattle around for a while as they are released from our collective consciousness. New leaders are emerging – torchbearers for the new more enlightened age ahead – and many people are working with nature and the elementals to help release the disturbance that our current way of living on the planet has caused. Some are working in fields such as agriculture, architecture, economics, science, medicine, metaphysics, politics and psychology, to help herald in the new and transform the old. It may seem a slow process but things are speeding up and dramatic shifts will inevitably happen.

There are now many awakened souls incarnate on the planet who are able to channel a very high vibration of light through their energy fields in order to build a grid of light within and around the planet. There are now being born – and about to be born – a great number of souls that are called 'Indigo children', who will bring many new gifts and abilities that have not been available on earth before. They will be born into every society and will help to anchor new qualities of love and joy on earth and assist in the changeover of the ages.

Within the next few decades many amazing events will occur. There will also be a certain amount of chaos and confusion since, at a personal and global level, many of the old ways of doing things will no longer work and many things will have to change or disappear. We are heading for an unimaginable shift in consciousness and this will lead to dramatic change in the outer world. Spirit is now sending impulses of light across our solar system, enabling us to wake up from the drowsiness of the Piscean age. Life cannot continue in the same way for much longer. If we are to make the transition to the fourth dimension it is inevitable that many social institutions and structures must also change, as must our attitudes towards ecology and our use of the earth's resources. It appears that some places in the world are getting much darker, in the sense that issues such as poverty, economic injustices, human rights, conflicts and terrorism are rising to the surface to be resolved and transformed.

At another level this global shift is causing many people to simplify their lives and re-evaluate what is meaningful. All the many splits that were created during the Piscean age – such as those between spirit and matter, the individual and the community, work and play, money and spirituality – are now coming to the surface to be healed. Many people are making the transition in their lives from a third-dimensional consciousness to a fourth-dimensional consciousness. In practical terms this means they are releasing suffering as a core method of growth and opening to grow through connectedness and joy and by following their dreams and the path of the heart. This cannot help but affect the very fabric of our collective daily reality, for every slight change we make towards being more loving and caring will have a tremendous impact on the planet. As we work to clear past-life contracts, negative patterns and limiting karmic bonds, we can open to greater and greater impulses of unconditional love from spirit and dissolve the illusion fear has wrapped around us. When the love vibration has been anchored, many new opportunities will open as old doors close. There may then be a pull to change or simplify our lifestyle as well as a need to explore new things that we might not have been interested in before. This process of transition to a fourth-dimensional consciousness will likely result in some challenging situations which will test our resolve and help clear any lingering doubts we may have about leaving the old behind. Our chakras above and beyond the crown centre are being gently opened and waves of light are pulsing down from spirit to be absorbed within our personality selves. This will help us to change from being personality centred to soul centred, which will allow the Higher Self to have more influence in our lives.

Everyone's path is unique, just as everyone's dream of heaven on earth is unique, so we must have courage and follow our heart and not be deflected from our course, no matter what challenges appear before us. We are in a time where every day the old energies of Pisces are being released and the new energies of Aquarius are being anchored into many of the structures that support how we live on the planet. The age of the dysfunctional and independent Piscean-age person struggling on all alone is fast approaching its final curtain. More and more it is important to network and co-operate with other like-minded people who can support our growth. This support network could be called a spiritual family, containing people who are alive now and those from the spirit realms.

We can leave the influence of the Age of Pisces when we are ready to make the transition; we do not have to wait for a specific time since the energies of Aquarius are available now. Awakening to this new energy may initially feel like having a foot in two worlds, one in the world of spirit and another in the everyday world. In time magic and miracles may begin to permeate our everyday life and the physical world will no longer appear so separate from the spiritual dimensions. We are now on the crest of a wave of change – and this may seem either very exciting or frightening, depending on your point of view. In this time of opportunity there is also danger, yet it seems less and less likely that many of the doom and gloom prophecies about this time will occur. Many metaphysical teachers are saying that Armageddon will not happen because we have made a collective choice to step into the fourth dimension, although some people may create realities of horror and destruction in their own lives. Aquarius has not fully kicked into existence yet, but it is going through the birthing process and many of us are helping in this. Many beings in the spiritual dimensions are also helping us to make the transition safely and smoothly.

## Meeting the Spirit of Aquarius

*Sit in silence and become very still using the awareness of the breath. In this stillness turn within and gently open your inner senses.*

*Breathe in light and allow this light to swirl around you in a gentle mist. Step through this mist and become aware of yourself standing on one side of a wide ravine, which is straddled by a great golden bridge. Your side of the ravine represents you standing in the energy of the Piscean age with all its fading energies of martyrdom, religion, struggle and suffering. How does it feel to stand on this side of the ravine? The other side of the ravine represents your future in the Aquarian age with all its new energies of co-operation, connectedness and emerging spirituality. How appealing does that side of the ravine feel?*

*If you are ready to release the Age of Pisces and move into Aquarius then begin to step on to the bridge. How smoothly can you pass across? Is there anything that appears to block your way? If so, find a way to pass through that block. If the block appears as a living being, see if you can reason with it and persuade it that stepping across will greatly enhance your life. You may have fear and doubt that this being wants to express to you. If the block appears as an inanimate object such as a net or wall, then simply find creative ways to pass through. It may be that no block appears at all.*

*When on the other side look back at the landscape you have left behind. If you are ready, ask spirit to dissolve the bridge so that you can let go of being centred in the fading energy of Pisces. You can choose not to do this at this time; you might want to straddle both energies for a while before severing your ties with the old one.*

*Somewhere in this new landscape is the angel that is overseeing*

*the dawning of this new age. Go now and look for this being;*
*perhaps you will meet him/her in a sacred temple, perhaps near a*
*beautiful waterfall or maybe beside a crystal-clear lake. Go now*
*and bask in the light of this being and ask it to anchor the energies*
*of the new age in your energy fields and within the cells of your*
*physical body. Allow its energy to permeate your emotions and*
*mind. Stay and enjoy this place for as long as you wish and then,*
*when you are ready, either return across the bridge or simply stay*
*in the landscape of Aquarius and from there come back to your*
*cycle of breath and your body.*

## Growth and Spirit

> *I slept and dreamt that life was joy,*
>
> *I awoke and saw that life was service*
>
> *I acted and behold, service was joy.*

Rabindranath Tagore

We have entered a time of rapid growth and in this window of opportunity spirit is assisting our growth through dreams, sudden intuitive flashes, bursts of inspiration, and synchronicity. Spirit is sending messages now via the intuitive or 'right brain' side and it is important to develop a balanced consciousness so that this flow of guidance is not impeded. As growth occurs through the polarities of joy and suffering, spirit will use either to help us grow, but if we are to take the next step we need more and more to release growth through suffering. And we have a choice – we can keep on struggling and suffering or we can learn the lesson of suffering, which is to let it go. Humanity has explored the polarity of suffering for some thousands of years, but its days as our primary path of growth are now numbered.

Resisting growth is like trying to cling to a safe harbour where the irresistible pull of the ocean, for a while, is kept at bay. Eventually we will surrender to the call of the ocean, whether in this lifetime or another, for in clinging we risk dying of boredom. To help us let go and discover new shorelines of possibility there are countless teachers in spirit who have walked the path before us and who will whisper to us at the times in our lives when we are listening intently. This can be in the stillness of meditation or when walking in a beautiful tranquil landscape in nature or, alternatively, when we are in crisis and calling out for help.

Growth leads us to that ravine that appears to divide the worlds of love and fear. The community of light beings is calling us to come and join them. Now is the time to heal the split between the worlds and in our own psyche. We can now learn that growth can be fun and that we are truly the beloved children of the universe.

## Changing Your Vibration

*Having a high vibration means living in the heart and being centred in a loving and peaceful space. In this place you are closer to the vibration of spirit where miracles can happen.*

*What activities or people leave you feeling depressed, depleted, worried, or anxious? What thoughts or nightmare scenarios haunt you? All these negative areas help to lower your vibration. Can you make new choices so that you can lift your vibration in these areas?*

*What activities or people help you feel more creative, energised, happy, joyful, inspired or tranquil? What dreams or visions inspire you? These positive areas help to raise your vibration, so choose to spend more time with them.*

## Changing Your Vibration as a Gift to the Planet

*Sit in meditation and come to your centre using your awareness of the cycle of the breath.*

*With each breath imagine your spine is drawing in light from the universe. As your spine grows in power it begins to extend up into the cosmos and down into the earth, like a pillar of light connecting you to heaven and earth.*

*From above your head a great ball of light descends until it is about 2–3 feet (60–90 centimetres) above the crown. This ball of light is your Star Chakra, and it radiates a golden-white light. Welcome this light. After a while you will feel a ball of light rising up from beneath the earth. It will begin to radiate an earthlight, of perhaps a bronze or reddish colour. This is your Earth Chakra and it comes to rest a few feet beneath you.*

*These two spheres pulse light to each other and enjoy a natural harmony. Between these two chakras the whole of your body is filled with light and energy. The two chakras form a circuit of power, and energy flows along your spine from these two points. This light can help clear any blocks that exist within the channel of your spine; simply ask that any blocks be dissolved in this flow of energy and light.*

*You can change the vibration of any part of yourself or a situation by holding in your awareness the flow between the two chakras and what you want this energy to resonate with. Sit in this flow and allow it to raise the vibration of your auric field.*

*When you are ready, return to your cycle of breath and full waking consciousness.*

*(The Earth Chakra is the seat of kundalini energy, which will rise in its own time. This energy need not be forced; it will rise in accordance with each individual's path of growth. The Star Chakra*

*is the gateway to higher consciousness and receives the impulses of
higher energy flow from the sun and the stars. This chakra will
respond to meditation and open to its fullest extent in its own
time.)*

## Service

Spiritual growth inevitably leads us to the path of service since we are
opening to a quality of love that naturally seeks to flow to others. As
we become more immersed in the light of spirit we lift our vibration
to a new finer level and as a result tend to become less and less
interested in all the drama, struggle and suffering that is
unconsciously generated in the world. This does not mean we lose
compassion, merely that we become more interested in and focused
on what is working. This is because through having loving
relationships, living prosperously, being creative and of service to
others, we are sending out a different note to the world and helping
to anchor the qualities of the fourth dimension. Many beings before
us have walked the path of service and illuminated the way for our
growth, and we in turn will become torchbearers for others. Our gift
to the planet is our decision to awaken, and everyone who chooses to
do this will play a part in the turning of the ages. Each act of love and
kindness can ripple out into the world and have untold effects. A
word of encouragement, a random act of kindness, a simple smile to
a stranger, a gift from the heart, all can touch many souls who in turn
may pass on your generosity to others. Begin to broadcast on the love
channel and radiate joy, fun tranquillity and humour to others, and
turn off the fear channel. This is a sure way to be of service and
improve your quality of living. Engage in some kind of spiritual
practice and find the time to meditate. From time to time step away
from the busyness of the world and open to being a channel of light.
Connect with the unseen friends and allow them to help you awaken

latent soul qualities and let your soul soar. This world needs you and needs what you can do for it.

## Service and Becoming a Spiritual Warrior

In ancient times leaders of the various tribes made pledges to honour and protect the land. Now that eco-systems are being thrown out of balance and disharmony ripples throughout the web, the planet needs spiritual warriors to stand up and work to heal and protect it. The earth cannot tolerate for much longer the harm that humanity is wreaking upon it. The great civilisation of Atlantis, forerunner of the civilisations of ancient India, Egypt and Central and South America, eventually reached a crisis similar to that facing us now – an epidemic of negative ego issues combined with the availability of powerfully destructive technology. Atlantis was destroyed by fire and water over 12,000 years ago and, according to some metaphysical teachers, many Atlantean souls are now reincarnated on the earth to ensure that we will not share the same fate. Many beings in spirit are focusing their energies upon the earth, and we can also receive help from our star brothers and sisters. We are in a time of transition, and this period of birthing may not be an easy one for many – and the ride is likely to be increasingly bumpy as we pass through the next few decades. One of the ways to help make it a smoother transition is to become a spiritual warrior, which means placing yourself in a position of service to spirit. The spiritual warrior surrenders the Conscious Self to the Higher Self and opens to the community of light beings. This act of surrender means you are making a choice to serve with spirit and become a guardian of the earth. Although much good work is being done in the outer world to protect the environment and all the ecosystems, what is also needed is work with meditation to send out healing vibrations to the web of life. Being a spiritual warrior does not entail fighting against anyone or anything; rather, it means making the decision to be a force for change in the world and to work for the healing of all its kingdoms. Many souls are now making the choice to serve the earth and are working with magic to heal and regenerate the web. This inner work will bring about much change in the outer world.

## The Return of the Goddess

*O Thou who gives sustenance to the Universe,*

*From Whom all things proceed,*

*And to Whom all things return,*

*Unveil to us the face of the true Spiritual Sun,*

*Hidden by a disc of golden light,*

*That we may know the truth,*

*And do our whole duty*

*As we journey to Thy Sacred Feet.*

Gayatri mantra

For thousands of years the balance of our planet has been disturbed by the loss of the Goddess principle. This loss happened gradually with the establishment of religions that imposed a strictly male deity. As the Goddess was banished or her role reduced in importance, the Divine began to be seen more and more as a father figure who would often be angry with his children and even punish them severely if they disobeyed the rules he imposed on his cosmos. As the Creator became increasingly seen as exclusively male, all spheres of power – from religion to the corporate and political arenas – became dominated by the masculine principle. Certain qualities that were labelled masculine became highly prized and other qualities that were labelled feminine became unfashionable and not highly valued. A split arose in the collective consciousness between spirit and matter, with the former becoming identified as masculine and the latter feminine. Consequently the earth was no longer seen as beautiful and sacred but as something to be used and exploited. With the loss of the feminine face of the Divine humanity collectively began to value the feminine principle less. Therefore women became more and more associated with the role of servitude in society and men came to be valued for their aggressive abilities. Without the guiding principle of the Priestess the Warrior was employed in finding ever more efficient ways to slaughter enemies on the battlefield. The scale of the rage and pain this has caused over the last several thousand years is unimaginable. Women have only recently been able to make much headway in finding equality in our world, and then it is usually only those with strong Warrior minds. The feminine face of God has been banished by most of the religions of our world, yet as we step into Aquarius she is returning. She comes to sweep away all limiting structures from our planet and to restore harmony in the outer and inner worlds. She is the face of the Spirit of All Things that has been ignored for thousands of years. Her shrines have been dishonoured and her followers have been vanquished. She comes to disrupt the unholy frameworks that seek to enslave the consciousness of humanity and she brings chaos to all systems of control and domination. Magic and sacred sexuality come trailing behind her as she returns to herald the dawning of the Age of Aquarius. She is calling all the unseen friends in the spirit realms to help her reweave all the broken strands of feminine energy within the web of life. As she returns, waves of angelic helpers are flooding the planet and many people are stepping forward to teach us how to work creatively with these beings. She comes to bring change and balance to the world, not a return to matriarchy. Her return does not mean that the Divine Masculine will be sidelined; rather, he will take his rightful place alongside the Divine Feminine. She comes to liberate not just women but also men from the systems of cruelty, repression and domination that are now ripe for collapse or transformation. The Divine Feminine is not separate from the Divine Masculine but is the other face of God. We live in a world that has been unbalanced for so long in terms of masculine and feminine energy that only the return of the Divine Feminine can restore harmony to the web.

It is no coincidence that mainly women attend most of the 'new age' workshops and that most of the healers and therapists around now are women. The Goddess was worshipped of old under many names, and each one was merely a facet of the great mystery. The Spirit of All Things is a being that is so beyond our comprehension that to know the totality of such a being was considered impossible. Our ancestors devised ways to know the Spirit of All Things through the creation of whole pantheons of gods and goddesses, where each being represented one or several qualities of the One and could be called upon for help. She was known by many names: Hera, Artemis and Aphrodite to the ancient Greeks; Bast, Isis, Nephthys, Sekmet and Hathor to the ancient Egyptians; and Arionrhod, Brigit and Ceridwen to the Celts of Europe. The monotheistic religions could have performed a great service had they not sought to vanquish the many-faced One and impose a tollbooth across the path of truth.

In the ancient tradition of Tantra, the kundalini is seen as a sleeping serpent that lies coiled within our Earth chakras. This feminine energy is now being roused from her slumber by the energies of Aquarius. When awakened through spiritual practice this goddess climbs up through the chakras, piercing each one along the way until she reaches the Brow Chakra where her journey is complete. Once she touches the brow her host will awaken to what has been called enlightenment. The goddess of kundalini energy is now rising within the collective psyche of humanity. She comes in many other guises in her bid to liberate and purify us in preparation for a new world. She comes as Aphrodite to liberate us from sexual tyranny, and as she awakens there will be a return to love and pleasure within romantic relationships and a return to the sacred act of lovemaking. She comes as Isis (the master of magic) to put back together the body of her beloved (the world) and restore it to life. She comes to pierce the veils of Piscean ignorance. She also comes as Kali, the Goddess of Destruction, to destroy the old so that the garden is weeded and prepared for the new.

## Meeting the Goddess of the Earth

*This is a journey to meet the Spirit of All Things as it expresses itself as the Goddess of the Earth. This involves making a commitment to honour the earth and all living beings upon it. It is a commitment to remain true to yourself and true to the web of life. If you are ready to make this commitment then enter into this journey now, otherwise wait until you feel in your heart that you are ready.*

*Once again connect with the cycle of breath and find your quiet centre. Release all attachment to the outer world and imagine you are breathing light into your heart. Feel this light calm your body, emotions and mind.*

*Open your inner senses and find yourself in a beautiful garden. Notice that this garden is full of wonderful red roses. Wander around and savour the scent of these flowers. This is a very earthy garden – feel its power and breathe in the redness of these roses. This garden lies at the bottom of a gentle hill and in the distance you can see many other gardens leading up to a temple of clear quartz crystal shimmering in the sunlight at the top of the hill. Stay in this garden of red flowers for a while and then notice a gate that leads to another garden further up the hill.*

*Pass through this gate and there you will find a garden full of orange flowers. Also in this garden are fountains of water and ponds filled with large orange-coloured fish. Breathe in the orange colour of these flowers. Stay here a while and then notice a gate that leads to another garden further up the hill.*

*This new garden is full of bright-yellow roses. Explore this garden and take in the scent of the flowers. This garden is also filled with gorgeous pale-yellow butterflies. Feel the excitement of these little beings and breathe in the yellow of these roses. Stay here a while and then notice that in this garden is a gate that leads to yet another garden further up the hill.*

*Enter this new garden and discover a garden full of greenery and bushes bursting with green buds waiting to open. Notice around the garden other green plants such as ivy and herbs. In this garden is a statue of Pan playing his pipes. Explore this garden and take in the scent of the herbs and fill yourself with the colour green. Stay here a while and then notice that in this garden is a gate that leads to another garden further up the hill.*

*Go through the gate and find yourself in a garden full of light-blue flowers with many different exotic scents. In this garden there are many bright-blue ribbons tied to the branches of small trees and these flutter in the wind. Breathe in the colour blue in this place and eventually you will find the gate that leads to the next garden further up the hill.*

*The temple of shimmering crystal is now much closer and you can see it as you step into the next garden of deeper-blue flowers. Here are many large and beautiful blue lapis crystals that have been carved into different figures. Breathe in the smells here and then pass into the final garden that surrounds the temple.*

*This last garden is filled with violet flowers and has large uncut amethyst crystals, in some places several feet tall. In this garden you are at the steps of the Crystal Temple. Pass through the flowerbeds and stand before the temple steps and breathe in the violet colour of the garden. Look down at yourself and see that you have breathed in the colours of the rainbow and your aura is shimmering like a rainbow.*

*Step into the temple and pass through its corridors to find its central chamber. There you will find in its centre an altar dedicated to the Goddess of the Green and Blue Earth. This room is shimmering with the power of the earth, and you can feel this power. Above your head sunlight cascades down through a clear quartz crystal ceiling.*

*Sit here for a while and drink in the power, and when you are ready begin to speak out your pledge of service to the earth. Stay in this temple and feel the presence of the Goddess of the Green and Blue Earth. She may take a human form and appear to you or she may remain within the structure of the temple listening to your pledge. Feel her love for you and open your heart to her. Listen now and hear her words of compassion and encouragement. She may leave a gift in the room for you. If so, take it and imagine absorbing its energy into your body.*

*Stay here as long as you wish, then when you are ready go back through all the gardens to the one at the bottom of the hill. Return to your body and to full waking consciousness.*

# The Great Migration

*Waiting, with only a glimpse of knowing,*
*It was often lonely, seemed long and possibly too late*
*Yet in the drumming of the Earth's heartbeat,*
*Crashing waves, rain on dry ground,*
*We heard the calling.*

*From the distant mountains, the vast plains,*
*From the choking desert sands and from the deep*
*Green valleys of contentment, we were summoned.*
*Reading the signs in rock pools and volcanoes,*
*Rainbows and scudding clouds giving directions,*
*We were observed scanning the horizons*
*For others of our kind.*

*At last, and often in some unlikely market-place,*
*There came a tentative nod of recognition.*
*Words shot like stars across a night sky*
*And our vision cleared as we joined the great migration.*

*Our clan, humankind, is on the move*
*From one point of understanding to the next.*
*We traverse the inner landscape to make new our world out there*
*The journey told in many tongues, changes with telling.*

*But we know, who see wind-worn beckoning trees,*
*Read pictures carved on rock faces and hear*
*The old ocean's rage and murmur,*
*We know the illusion of separation.*

*And we sing, our own song, yet the One song,*
*With joy, loudly now we sing.*

Susan Hill

# GLOSSARY

**Angel** – a guiding or 'architect' consciousness that can be found at work here on the earth guiding the mineral, plant, animal and human kingdoms. They are found in all the planes of existence working with the Spirit of All Things to assist the unfolding evolution of all life.

**Basic Self** – one of the layers of consciousness known in the wisdom of Huna. This self is the physical/emotional self that has the capacity of memory. It is our vulnerable, playful and spontaneous Inner Child Self.

**Chakra** – a disc-like vortex centre of energy that forms where the greatest number of energy lines converges within the etheric body. There are seven major chakras in the body, connected by a central vertical channel called the Susumna. There are also many minor centres around the body, such as in the palms of the hands and soles of the feet.

**Conscious Self** – one of the layers of consciousness known in the wisdom of Huna. This self has the capacity of speech, intuition, intelligence and action. This is the part we most identify with.

**Earth plane** – the place of physical birth, death and action. Here we grow through a spectrum of challenges set up within the principle of polarity. The 'lesser builders' maintain this plane of existence under the guidance of the 'architect' angelic beings.

**Elementals** – those tiny beings that are the 'lesser builders' of form within the physical world. They are also to be found working within the emotional and mental realms. These are the beings of earth, air, fire and water – and also of spirit (the latter transmit life-force energy). All these beings work under the guidance of the angelic presence.

**Energy** – defined in the *Oxford English Dictionary* as 'the capacity for activity, force and vigour. The ability of matter or radiation to do work'. In this book energy has a broader definition for it refers not only to the body but also to the emotions, the etheric body, the mind and life-force energy (or prana) that radiates through the cosmos from our sun.

**Etheric body** – our energy body that sits within and surrounds the physical body. It assimilates life-force energy from the cosmos via the chakras, and it is here that the blueprint which enables the body to be continually constructed and maintained is held. The etheric body is filled with channels that distribute life force around the physical body, which is where illness or wellbeing is generated. The etheric body is governed by the Basic Self.

**Evolution** – physical evolution is defined in the *Oxford English Dictionary* as 'the origination of species by development from earlier forms, not by special creation'. Evolution in this book has a much broader meaning since it includes the evolution or growth of the entire human being, including not only the physical body but also the emotional, mental and spiritual.

**False Self** (also known as the negative ego) – the part of our personality that seeks to defend our vulnerability as our conscious mind is forming. This part contains all the criticism, hatred, doubt, fear, judgement and self-attack we have ever experienced. Its main objective is to keep us safe and it will do this even if has to kill us in the process. This part will suppress and keep at bay any bit of us it considers harmful. It is the polar twin of the Shadow and as such is the greatest obstacle on our path of growth.

**Fourth dimension** – a term used to describe the state of being a heart-centred being who experiences a reality that is fundamentally loving and supportive.

**Higher Self** – one of the layers of consciousness known in the wisdom of Huna. This self is the guardian angel of the psyche; it motivates and guides all the other selves in their growth.

**Inner planes** – planes other than the physical plane of existence. The emotional or astral plane is the sphere of desire and feeling, the mental plane is the sphere of the mind and all of its formations, and the spiritual planes are the home of our Higher Self and other beings.

**Intuition** – a synergistic inner ability to understand or know information. It comes from our innate connectedness with all life. Intuition is felt and known through the physical body, the feelings and the mind.

**Karma** – the continual cycle of cause and effect which leads us to reap the consequences of our past actions. This is an aspect of growth and has nothing to do with divine punishment or reward; it is a principle of how the universe operates, just like the law of gravity.

**Kundalini** – the serpent goddess who slumbers in the Earth Chakra below our feet. At a certain point in our evolution she awakens and climbs the vertical channel connecting the chakras, piercing each one on her way to the Brow Chakra, where she awakens her host to a new state of consciousness.

**Ley lines** – energy pathways within the etheric body of the earth, similar to the lines of energy in our own etheric bodies. Sacred sites usually have many ley lines converging upon them.

**Life-force energy** – (prana in India, chi in China, ki in Japan, mana in Hawaii) – energy absorbed by the body through food, the breath and sunlight.

**Magic** – the art of utilising the innate abilities of consciousness to call upon the unseen forces and intelligence in the universe to help influence and shape events and circumstances on the physical plane.

**Power animal** – the guiding consciousness that works with a whole species of animal such as bear or fox. Such guiding beings are a part of the angelic kingdom.

**Priestess (Inner)** – the anima or inner feminine aspect of our consciousness. This part is receptive, inward looking, intuitive, connected, and is able to communicate with the Basic Self. It is seated in the right hemisphere of the brain.

**Psyche** – defined in the *Oxford English Dictionary* as 'the human soul or spirit; the human mind'. I define it as the container of all that we can be and all that we can become. It is a thought in the mind of the Spirit of All Things.

**Ritual** – a ceremony with a clearly defined purpose that can mark a rite of passage in life or be used to celebrate a sacred time of the year or an event. Ritual can also be used to connect more meaningfully with spirit, or to manifest an intent. It usually employs rhythmic music or chanting in order to gain the attention of the Basic Self so that the door to spirit is opened. Rituals have been used for thousands of years in indigenous cultures across the world.

**Shadow** – the container of the parts of our emerging consciousness that are discarded or disowned as we grow up. The shadow is the most hidden and unconscious part of the Basic Self. It holds these positive or negative parts of our consciousness until we are ready to accept them back again. This part is our ally on our path of growth and is the polar twin of the False Self

**Soul** – within the psyche the part of us that contains all the experiences of what has been. It is our place of pure being.

**Spirit** – within the psyche the part of us that yearns to stretch into new possibilities. It is the place that calls to us to become something more.

**The path of the heart** – the direction in life that is most in accord with the reasons for our incarnation, the essence of what we came to earth to do and be.

**The Spirit of All Things** – another term for the Creator and Sustainer of All Life or the sponsoring consciousness that gives rise to all life. The process of growth begins when we separate from this source and ends when we return to the source of our existence.

**The Web of All Things** – a term to describe the etheric energy web that links all living creatures and forms. The web is a shamanic term describing our innate state of interconnectedness.

**Unseen friends** – a collective term for all the spirit guides and teachers who are willing and ready to be of assistance to humanity.

**Warrior (Inner)** – the animus or inner masculine aspect of our consciousness. This part is active, dynamic, outward looking; it uses the intellect to separate and understand and is able to protect the vulnerability of the Basic Self. It is seated in the left hemisphere of the brain.

**Yin/Yang** – a concept of Chinese philosophy that saw the whole universe in a dance of opposite yet complementary tendencies ever seeking balance and harmony. Yin is the reflective and passive principle, yang the active and thrusting principle.

# FURTHER READING

Anand, Margot, *The Art of Sexual Magic,* Piatkus, 1995

Andrews, Ted, *How to Meet and Work with Spirit Guides,* Llewellyn, 2000

Bradshaw, John, *Home Coming,* Piatkus, 1990

Bailey, Alice, *Letters on Occult Meditation,* Lucis, 1922

Bailey, Alice, *A Treatise on Cosmic Fire,* Lucis, 1951

Bailey, Alice, *A Treatise on White Magic,* Lucis, 1934

Bloom, William (ed.), *Penguin Book of the New Age,* Penguin, 2001

Branden, Nathaniel, *Six Pillars of Self Esteem,* Bantam, 1994

Capra, Fritjof, *The Tao of Physics,* Flamingo, 1975

Capra, Fritjof, *The Web of Life,* Anchor, 1996

Carr-Gomm, Philip and Stephanie, *The Druid Animal Oracle,* Connections, 1996

Coles, Robert, *The Erik Erikson Reader,* Norton, 2000

Cooper, Diana, *Angel Inspiration,* Hodder, 2001

Cooper, Diana, *A Little Light on Ascension,* Findhorn, 1997

Daniel, Alma, Timothy Wyllie, and Andrew Ramer, *Ask Your Angels,* Piatkus, 1992

Dewey, Barbara, *As You Believe,* Bartholomew Books, 1985

Edwards, Gill, *Living Magically,* Piatkus, 1991

Edwards, Gill, *Pure Bliss,* Piatkus, 1999

Edwards, Gill, *Stepping Into the Magic,* Piatkus, 1993

Gifford, Jane, *The Celtic Wisdom of Trees,* Godsfield Press, 2000

Hoffman, Enid, *Huna – A Beginner's Guide,* Whiteford Press, 1976

Holden, Robert, *Shift Happens!,* Hodder, 2000

Ingerman, Sandra, *Soul Retrieval,* Harper Collins, 1991

Judith, Anodea, *The Wheels of Life,* Llewellyn, 1996

Kenton, Leslie, *Journey to Freedom,* Thorsens, 1998

Kindred, Glennie, *Sacred Celebrations,* Gothic Image, 2001

King, Serge Kahili, *Mastering Your Hidden Self,* Quest, 1985

King, Serge Kahili, *The Urban Shaman,* Simon & Schuster, 1990

Krystal, Phyllis, *Cutting the Ties That Bind,* Samuel Weiser, 1993

Lazaris, *The Sacred Journey: You and Your Higher Self,*
   NPM Publishing, 1987

Linn, Denise, *Sacred Space,* Rider, 1995

Matthews, Caitlin, *Singing the Soul Back Home,* Element, 1995

McCrickard, Janet, *Eclipse of the Sun,* Gothic Image, 1990

Osho, *Meditation: The First and Last Freedom,* Boxtree, 1995

Peck, M. Scott, *The Road Less Travelled,* Arrow, 1990

Puttick, Liz, *Women in New Religions,* Macmillan, 1997

Reyo, Zulmo, *Mastery: The Path of Inner Alchemy,* Janus, 1994

Roberts, Jane, *The Individual and the Nature of Mass Events (A Seth
   Book),* Prentice-Hall, 1981

Roberts, Jane, *The Nature of Personal Reality (A Seth Book),* Amber
   Allen, 1995

Roman, Sanaya, *Living with Joy,* Kramer, 1986

Roman, Sanaya, *Personal Power Through Awareness,* Kramer, 1986

Roman, Sanaya, *Spiritual Growth,* Kramer, 1989

Sams, Jamie, and David Carson, *Medicine Cards,* Bear & Co., 1988

Shapiro, Debbie, *Your Body Speaks Your Mind,* Piatkus, 1996

Starhawk, *The Spiral Dance,* HarperCollins, 1979

Starhawk, *Truth or Dare,* HarperCollins, 1987

Stone, Hal, and Sidra Winkelman, *Embracing Our Selves,* New World Library, 1989

Thich Nhat Hanh, *The Heart of the Buddha's Teaching,* Rider, 1999

Walsh, Neale Donald, *Conversations with God,* Book 1, Hodder, 1995

Wanless, James, *Voyager Tarot,* Merrill-West, 1989

Williams, Nick, *The Work We Were Born To Do,* Element, 1999

Wolfe, Amber, *In the Shadow of the Shaman,* Llewellyn, 1995

Ziegler, Gerd, *Tarot, Mirror of the Soul,* Samuel Weiser, 1985

# RESOURCES

For information on materials supporting this book (such as meditation CDs and affirmation cards) please visit www.freeingthespirit.co.uk or write to:

Spirit Trails
23 Dornden Drive
Langton Green
Kent TN3 0AA

For information on events run by Steve Nobel please check the above website or write to:

Steve Nobel
Freeing the Spirit
c/o Alternatives
St James Church
197 Piccadilly
London W1J 9LL

If you wish to contact Steve Nobel please write to him c/o Alternatives or email freeingthespirit@yahoo.co.uk

# USEFUL ADDRESSES

I can recommend all of the following people or organisations, having personally been involved with them or experienced their work. Contact them direct for further details and information on events.

## UK
### GENERAL

Alternatives
St James's Church
197 Piccadilly
London W1J 9LL
Tel: 020 7287 6711
alternatives@ukonline.co.uk
www.alternatives.org.uk

College of Psychic Studies
16 Queensbury Place
London SW7 2EB
Tel: 0207 589 3292
www.psychic-studies.org.uk

Findhorn Foundation
Forres IV36 3TZ
Scotland
Tel: 01309 691653
www.findhorn.org

Life Times in Reading
Tel: 0118 926 4378
www.life-times.co.uk

## SHAMANISM AND EARTH SPIRITUALITY

British Reclaiming Witchcamps
Tel: 0208 667 1525
camp@reclaim.demon.co.uk

Children of Artemis
www.witchcraft.org

Eagles Wing Centre for
Contemporary Shamanism
Tel: 01435 810233
www.shamanism.co.uk

Sacred Trust
Tel: 01225 852615
www.sacredtrust.org

Vision Quests in Britain
(Kent area)
www.spirittrails.co.uk

## Inspiration and Personal Development

Core Energy Management
(William Bloom)
Tel: 01372 272400
www.williambloom.com

Diamond Light Tantra
Tel: 08700 780584
www.diamondlighttantra.com

Heart at Work Project
(Nick Williams)
Tel: 07000 781922
www.heartatwork.net

The Happiness Project
Tel: 01865 244414
www.happiness.co.uk

Insight Seminars UK
Tel: 02088 832 888
www.insight-seminars.org

## Metaphysics

Heaven on Earth
(Chris Sell)
Tel: 01434 322149
www.heaven-on-earth.co.uk

Living Magically (Gill Edwards)
Tel: 015394 31943
www.livingmagically.co.uk

Lucis Trust
(Alice Bailey)
Tel: 020 7839 4512
www.triangles.org

## Europe

Scandinavian Center for Shamanic Studies (Jonathan Horowitz)
(Also has information on events in UK)
Tel: 020 8459 3028
www.shaman-center.dk

## USA
### Metaphysics

Lazaris
www.lazaris.com

Orin and DaBen
www.orindaben.com

Seth
www.spiritual-endeavors.org/
seth/index.html
and www.sethnet.org/

## SHAMANISM AND EARTH SPIRITUALITY

Foundation for Shamanic Studies
(events all over)
www.shamanicstudies.com

Reclaiming Tradition of Witchcraft
(events all over)
www.reclaiming.org

Serge Kahili King (Hawaii)
www.huna.org

## INTERNATIONAL

Inspiration and Personal
Development
Insight Seminars Worldwide
www.insight-seminars.org

# INDEX

# Index